In Your Face

In Your Face

*What Facial Features
Reveal About the People
You Know and Love*

by

Bill Cordingley

New Horizon Press
Far Hills, New Jersey

New Horizon Press
P.O. Box 669
Far Hills, NJ 07931

Cordingley, Bill
      In Your Face: What Facial Features Reveal About the People
      You Know and Love

Interior Design: Susan M. Sanderson
Illustrations: Gail Tavares

Library of Congress Control Number: 00-132566

ISBN: 0-88282-201-2
New Horizon Press

Manufactured in the U.S.A.

2005   2004   2003   2002   2001   /   5   4   3   2   1

Dedication

Few interests in my life have been as long-lived as my fascination with reading faces. Few subjects have brought me more pleasure or better connected me with the people I've met. For this, I am profoundly grateful to Mazury O'Connell, the originator of this face reading method.

Mazury shared with me her dream of introducing the world to a new and useful way to connect with people. For many months she generously gave her time, shared her home and patiently taught and coached me, trusting that one day this book would emerge. I would not have been able to write a word of this volume without the knowledge, earnestness, patience, perseverance, extraordinary vision and loving support she offered.

Unfortunately, Mazury passed away in 1999. I regret she won't be able to enjoy the product of our long-time friendship and collaboration.

Table of Contents

Acknowledgements

This book has taken nearly three decades to write. In that time many people have contributed to it. Some have lent their individual talents to the project, while others have shared their thoughts and enthusiasm for it at critical times.

Above all, I want to acknowledge John and Cara Chisholm and their family. Not only did they introduce me to Mazury O'Connell, the originator of this powerful method, but they opened their hearts and home to me with their very special friendship. They also put me on the path toward authoring such a book and they believed in me long before I started to believe in myself.

I am greatly indebted to my friend Gail Tavares for enthusiastically and expertly creating dozens of illustrations that complement my words. I am equally thankful to Kate Lynch for generously offering her editorial comments and for keeping me focused on the fulfillment of my dream.

For their earnest encouragement over these many years, I also thank my friends Robert Thomases, Marj "Robinson" Lacy, Tom Cordingley, Connie Cordingley, David and Ellen Schaefer, Helen Cameron, Susan Heyden and Gary Howes, Alex and Pat Swistel, Rich Morris and Preston Black.

I'm truly honored to know and work with Abraham, Jerry and Esther Hicks, Sharon and Sam Gleason, Janey Schmohl, Karen Snyder, Mike Ambrosi, Kathleen Holland, Chuck Collison, Mary Maher, Terri-Lynn Cousley, Jackie Grace, Jan Sarvis and Alan Birnshein and I thank them for their ongoing, heartfelt support.

I want to thank Rich Vitaliano, my mentor, who helped me launch my career as a professional writer; David Hughes and "E" Sorenson for giving me my first writing job; Yvonne Jaffe, whose encouragement and counsel helped me overcome my self-doubt and led me to teach Psycho-Graphicology; and Chris Baker for sharing his perspectives as a published author. For their many varied individual words of encouragement and suggestions, I also thank Mike Garvey, Betsy, Eddie, Ed and Susan Cotter, David Galland, Grace Alexander, Lee Boyack, Margaret Woo, Larry Roellig, Mike and Donna Scippa, Dixie and Lynn Waldrip, Anna Shubeau, Nancy Kiskis, Sally Faith Dorfman, Jack Jacobs, Paul Spiegel, Ed Sigall, Barbara Malina and Scott Wachter.

I'm lucky enough to have an extraordinary agent, Laurie Harper. Instantly recognizing both the potential of my manuscript and the value of this face reading method, Laurie quickly became my single strongest advocate. I am very grateful for her tireless assistance and encouragement. I am also most thankful to my friends at New Horizon Press, talented people who were willing to take a chance on an atypical book dealing with an unusual subject from an unpublished author.

Above all, I want to thank my amazing wife, Pam, the woman whose face I read so long ago and decided was meant for me, and my three loving children, Will, Christina and Kaylie. In the twenty-plus years we have been together, Pam has been my champion, my guiding light, my conscience and often my strength. Ever supportive, she has tolerated me during countless hours when I struggled to translate this system to the written word and bring to light its inherent value. More than allowing me to pursue my passion, my family has actively encouraged me and has helped keep my inspiration alive. I truly could never have written this book without their boundless, loving support.

Preface

Sixty years ago, a young portrait artist named Mazury O'Connell stood at work behind her easel and chatted with a client. As her subject grumbled on about her difficult children, her temperamental husband and her unhappy life, something guided Mrs. O'Connell to observe the woman's mouth. She noted that both corners turned down, almost in a perpetual frown.

Suddenly, she came face to face with a question, the answer to which would forever alter her life: *What if our mouths were reliable indicators of how we view our lives?*

Over the following weeks, Mrs. O'Connell studied one portrait client after another, carefully observing how the shapes of their mouths correlated with their outlooks on life. The result? She saw an unmistakable pattern. When mouth corners turned down, those people were invariably pessimists. When they turned up, they were optimists. She found this to be true without exception. The correlations were unmistakable, the implications far-reaching and the next, bigger question was unavoidable: *What if our facial features are actually blueprints of who we really are and how we think?*

Over the next thirty years, on hundreds and hundreds of portrait clients, Mrs. O'Connell continued to observe the striking relationships between facial features and personality traits. By 1970, based solely on her study, Mrs. O'Connell had constructed an entire system of "reading" faces. She discovered the relationships between dozens of facial features and hundreds of distinct personality traits. Plus, she became so accurate in her assessments that her efforts were uniformly praised by her subjects.

In 1972, my good friend John, knowing I enjoyed writing, introduced me to Mrs. O'Connell. She wanted to write a book, he explained, and suggested that I might be interested in helping her.

I was game. Ever since I was a little boy, I had been intrigued by the hard-to-explain. I was fascinated by palmistry and astrology and studied handwriting analysis as a hobby. But, as interesting as these subjects were to me, I had no idea how mesmerized I would be by the fun, accuracy and usefulness of reading faces.

A moment after I stepped into her modest New England home, I caught Mrs. O'Connell quickly scanning my face and smiling broadly. Moments later, I discovered she absolutely knew who I was and what I was about. For forty-five minutes she "read" my face and pointed out dozens of aspects of my personality—my abilities, longings, innermost needs, behavior, attitudes and so much more. She knew without any doubt or hesitation an amazing amount about how I thought, how I felt, how I acted and what I needed to feel fulfilled. It was truly an extraordinary experience.

I had had enough experiences by that point in my life to know that many things she said were true. But she also told me about traits I had never attributed to myself. For example, she quickly studied my forehead, my chin and my nose and, with the greatest certainty, said "Bill, you could be an excellent writer, a good politician and a fine speaker." *I could?* I thought. *Really?*

She continued to focus on other promising qualities, including a number of traits and abilities I had certainly never given myself credit for having. She said I was a "genius with numbers" and capable of taking on vast responsibilities. She mentioned my intelligence, my diplomatic nature, my ability to take charge when I want to and my capacity to adjust to new situations easily.

Mrs. O'Connell pointed out career directions she said I would enjoy. She explained how I could read faces to better understand the people with whom I would deal. Most exciting of all—she told me how to spot women I'd enjoy meeting, just by knowing specific facial features to look for. What a concept!

We talked for hours. I was spellbound. I knew that almost everything she said was true. Absolutely true. I also knew that the only way she would have known *any* of those things was from my face...from the shape of my nose, the curve of my chin, the height of my forehead, the thickness of my neck. I was so convinced that I decided, then and there, to move to her town, work with her in my spare time and help her write her book.

I spent the following summer apprenticing with Mrs. O'Connell on Cape Cod. For three months I watched her amaze and

Introduction

Within thirty seconds of my first glimpse of my future wife Pam on a blind date, I knew more about this woman than her very closest friends. I knew she was someone I would enjoy and someone who had dozens of the qualities I was looking for in a life-long partner. Believe it or not, I knew all that from her face.

By looking at certain features of Pam's face, I was able to tell a great deal about what made her "tick." I knew many of her attitudes. I understood her needs (including her physical and romantic desires). I saw her likes and loves, her longings, her loathings, her dislikes, her drives and desires. I also had a good idea how she thought, how she acted and how she felt.

In short, I knew at a glance a great deal about Pam and I knew that she was someone I wanted to get to know much better. I was able to enter our relationship with my eyes wide open, really knowing the person I was dating. Today, some twenty-eight years later, we are still enjoying the companionship, respect and understanding that first glance predicted and have three lovely children.

One of the main reasons our lives have blended successfully is that I knew what I was looking for and how these traits expressed themselves in her face. Since I knew how to read faces, I genuinely *knew* that she was the woman I wanted to spend my life with—the very moment we met—and this made the development of a deep and meaningful relationship between us a faster, smoother, more rewarding experience.

You too can improve your chances of having similar successful relationships if you decide to spend just a little time learning how to uncover the secrets hidden in the facial features of those to whom you are attracted or with whom you wish to become friends. Face reading is a tool that will serve you well, now and in the future, wherever you are in life. It's a fun, productive and easy way in which you can learn to identify whether someone to whom you're attracted has personality traits you like or ones you don't. Plus, it helps you reduce the time it usually takes—months, sometimes years—to discover what your potential partner is *really* like and if she or he is the right person with whom to embark upon a future together.

Those are big promises, I know. But when we're finished with the amazing journey through the world of face reading that we're about to begin, you'll understand completely why I feel confident making such bold statements.

You Have Already Read Faces (But Not Like This)

When was the last time you met someone and knew *right away* that the two of you could be a good match?

It's a lot more likely that you have begun most of your romantic relationships fairly sure that you knew what your partner was like, only to find out weeks, months or even years later you didn't know him or her nearly as well as you thought you did.

We've all had experiences like that, probably throughout our dating lives. Why? Because we've come to believe that shared time and

Wouldn't you love to get a quick "read" on the people who are or you hope will be important in your life? The attractive guy or girl next door with the deep chin—affectionate or a cold fish? Your about-to-be fiance—does that broad forehead signal trouble ahead? You married him with that short, thick neck—now learn what it means.

experiences are the only ways to know what our partners and new friends are really like. But there is a much better way and I am about to describe it to you. This method of reading faces will give you additional skills that will enable you to select the right partners for yourself, be they mates, lovers or friends, without enduring the lengthy, difficult and often disappointment-filled process of choosing a partner in the usual hit-or-miss fashion. In these pages, I will teach you a simple, fast and highly accurate way to assess the real person behind the smile.

Imagine how useful (and fun) it would be to peer inside the well-polished facade of the people to whom you're attracted and see who they *really* are! Imagine being able to identify their strongest drives and most dominant needs. Wouldn't you love to know if their sex drive is compatible with yours? Or if their romantic inclinations and dominant attitudes match yours? How about their natural abilities, typical behaviors and core values? You can gather this information—within moments of meeting them—just from looking at their faces!

Does it seem odd to think a face could reveal so much? It shouldn't. Think about it. You *already* read faces. We all do it constantly. We continually evaluate people by studying their faces, their bodies, their gestures, their voices and more. And we use what we see (and hear) as a basis for drawing conclusions about them—often crucial, far-reaching conclusions.

Think of people you met recently for the first time. Didn't you immediately start sizing them up? Of course, we all do. We rely on others' appearances to help us decide whether we like them, if we trust them, plus all kinds of other assessments. We look at new acquaintances' faces and decide whether they're kind and gentle or critical and disapproving. We evaluate their senses of humor. We judge whether they're smart or not, assertive or withdrawn, friendly or unapproachable. We even decide if they're honest, trustworthy and sincere. That's a long list of important conclusions for just having met someone! But it shows that we assess people all the time...and we do it largely from their faces.

Have you noticed how we ascribe traits to certain facial features? We talk about people's "beady eyes," or their "pouting mouths," their "tight lips," "jolly cheeks" or their "bedroom eyes." Have you ever wondered why intellectual people are sometimes called "highbrow" and not-so-smart people are sometimes dubbed "pinheads"? Clearly, at some inner level, we know what people's faces are telling us about them.

That explains why, in one form or another, face reading has been around for ages. In Asia, people have been practicing varying forms of face reading for thousands of years. It's an accepted part of their culture. In the United States, we have had an on-again, off-again interest in the subject going back to the 1800s. Thankfully, today, our medical community is beginning to take an interest. In fact, in the tradition of eastern medicine, western science has just started considering the relationships between patients' faces and their health. For example, did you know that doctors now see a link between creases that appear on our earlobes and high blood pressure? I expect that they will look for and discover additional relationships of this kind in the future.

See the face, see the personality

What, exactly, do we see in a face to which we are attracted? Before we discuss the nuggets of information you can mine from a face, some definitions are in order.

By reading the entire face, a skilled person can map out an individual's *personality*. Here, we define personality as a unique set of basic, core traits with which each of us is born. These are the innate qualities which are part of us over the course of our lives. We use and develop many of them while attempting to ignore others. In the face reading system I use, we study sixty distinct *personality traits,* each with its own corresponding facial feature. At their core, almost all of these

> *Some people care a great deal about other people and their welfare. Is that the kind of person you want? Then look at his or her eyes. Are they very rounded on top? If so, you've found a caring individual.*

traits are fundamental needs or drives that people intuitively seek to satisfy, according to their intensity.

As you'll see, these drives and needs, in turn, have a lot to do with shaping our talents, abilities, actions, beliefs, expectations, limitations, thinking, behavior, preferences and tastes.

In other words, our faces display distinct pictorial evidence of our most dominant needs and drives, forces that continually shape how we act, how we communicate, how we feel, how we think and much more. For example, when we assess how far a woman's nose protrudes from her face, the depth of her chin, the width of her eye, the curve of her eyebrow or the height of her forehead, we are identifying many of the drives the person has—drives which motivate her to act in certain ways.

What's in his or her face?
When you are involved in the dating game, the question *"What's he really like?"* underlies those early meetings.

Want to know instantly if your prospective partner is likely to be genuine or if he or she is putting on an act? You will. How about being able to know who desires very physical relationships and who values more cerebral partners? You'll have the ability to see that, too. You'll also be able to spot stubborn, rigid people as well as those who are easy-going and flexible. You'll find out who likes to take risks and who's risk-averse...who's critical of other people and who is more accepting...who gets attached to people and dives headlong into relationships and who's likely to stay forever detached, distracted and aloof.

You truly are about to learn how to pierce just about anyone's exterior veneer and stare straight into their core being.

Is this a valuable skill? Of course! Revealing? Definitely! It's also easy to learn and can be practiced anywhere, anytime.

Once you have memorized this method of face reading, you will be able to immediately discern which of the men and women you meet are *simpatico* with you and which will make your best possible partners in life.

Answering the age-old question: Who is this person really?
You know the drill. You go out with someone with whom you enjoy spending time. You want the relationship to grow and thrive. At the

same time, the other person seems to like you, too. Yet you can't help but start asking yourself those nagging questions...

Is this really going to work? Is he really "the one"? Is he really as wonderful as he seems to be? Are we the great match we seem? Is she as caring as she appears? As loving? As fun? And what about the future? Will she be as attentive and affectionate next year as she is right now?

To sum it up: Is this person worth my time? Is he or she someone I can be with in a lasting, fulfilling relationship?

As you know, you don't get answers to questions like these quickly. You can't exactly expect the object of your affection to level with you about what she's really like. (*"Yes, dear, since you asked, I really am a very selfish, uncaring, stubborn person at heart."*) And it's just not good form to ask her friends what she's really like. So, what do we do?

> *Do you want to meet someone who's a good listener? The best listeners are people with long necks, especially thin, long necks. Do you love the way her mouth curves up at the corners? She's an optimist and may inspire an "up" attitude in you, too.*

We date. We "test drive" our potential partners, counting on time together and shared experiences to help us assess how good a match we really are.

My wife Pam and I dated for three years before we got married. We spent many days together and even lived together for six months before tying the knot. Even then, while *I knew her* thoroughly (from reading her face), Pam discovered after all that time that *she really didn't know me* nearly as well as she thought she did. She had fallen into the trap most people do: She didn't realize how well I was acting my part—I was being the person she wanted me to be. Would she have married me if she had been able to read my face and realize I'm very good at "putting on a front"? Yes, she says (thankfully). But she also says that, with her eyes completely open and seeing the real me, she might have approached our relationship differently.

We all put on fronts because we all want to make a good

impression on others. Who wouldn't? The problem is that we also want to believe that other people (who, like us, are trying to make a good impression) are just being themselves. We incorrectly assume that we're seeing who they really are.

Look at face reading as your chance to get to know the authentic person behind the smiling, "I'll-do-anything-for-you" face. You're about to learn valuable tools for assessing whether the person whose eyes you're blissfully gazing into (or want to gaze into) is the person you think he or she is or just another impostor.

In these pages, you'll discover the meaning and significance of twelve key facial features, each one revealing many important traits you need to know about a potential friend, lover or partner. You'll be able to identify his or her innermost needs, most influential beliefs, defining attitudes, behavioral tendencies, talents and abilities, plus many basic, powerful drives.

It's not magic, it's not psychic ability—it's face reading and it will give you an edge, an advantage in your romantic relationships that you've never dreamed possible.

How to prove it to yourself
Think of someone you know well—a teacher, parent, boss, friend or mate—whose nose has a pointed tip (see illustration below).

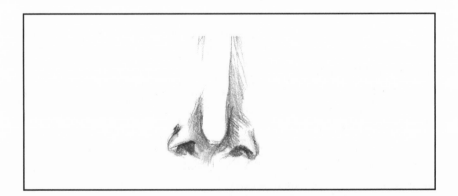

Unless he's also an extremely self-controlled person who can expertly hide his true self, I would bet money that you find this person very judgmental, even critical.

Now think of people you know with large, full lips in relation to the rest of their facial features (see illustration above). They probably enjoy receiving lots of attention and love interacting with others. How about people with proportionately thin lips? Haven't you found these people to be less outgoing?

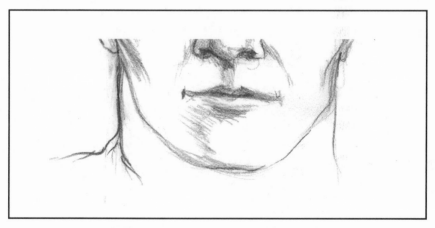

Finally, recall someone with a thick neck, especially a short one (see illustration above). Isn't he or she one of the most stubborn people you know?

Isn't that amazing? How can facial features reveal insights into someone's personality? How can the face have anything to do with how we think and feel and act?

That's a lot like asking how our palms (in palmistry) or the stars (in astrology) tell us about our personalities. Some would say you just have to accept that it works. That's partly true. But, at the same time, there are actually some good, scientifically based reasons why it works.

The best way—actually, the only way—to decide how well face reading works is to try it out yourself. Rather than reading through this entire book and learning all the facets before putting them to use, try a simpler approach:

Scan these pages for the particular facial features that intrigue you or belong to your friends or family members—people you already know well. Discover what they mean and then use them right away to analyze their personalities. You'll be amazed at the accuracy of your analyses.

A quick word of reassurance: Once you get proficient at reading faces, spotting these traits will be almost second nature. It'll be so natural, in fact, that you'll probably find yourself using it on many people every day. You'll find that reading faces is like having an extra set of eyes...you can't help but see and learn a whole lot more!

Get a Peek at That Special Person From the Inside-Out

When you can read faces, you discover what makes people "tick." There will no longer be such a thing as an ordinary face. Every face, every feature you see has meaning. Each one tells a story. Suddenly, you can pick up a magazine and instantly know a great deal about your favorite (and not-so-favorite) celebrities, political figures, business magnates and other famous people.

For years, I've enjoyed reading the faces of presidential and other political candidates. I've also studied famous historical figures to get a better sense of what personality traits they possessed that might have been responsible for their achievements.

On the lighter side, when two celebrities publicly announce they are involved in a relationship, I've been known to run out and buy magazines just so I could analyze their faces and compare and contrast their personalities. When you spot similar or complementary traits in two people, you can often tell in what ways they're best suited for each other. Likewise, when you spot key differences, the savvy face reader can anticipate aspects of their relationship that will probably give them trouble, even before they do.

It's time for you to glimpse a few of the many traits you can uncover from a face. To help you get started, we're going to do two brief analyses using photographs. Besides the personality insights themselves, you'll want to take note of a few important things:

- First, notice how helpful it would be to have insights like these about important people (especially that potential significant other) in your life!
- Observe how an experienced face reader can determine the importance and strength of a particular trait belonging to the subject.
- Notice the wide variety of personality traits you can uncover.
- See how different these two people are.
- Consider how these traits work both individually and in combination to influence each person's behavior and thinking.
- Finally, recognize that, even though you've never met these two people, their faces are shouting volumes of personal information about who they are—things you didn't know, *couldn't know*, before.

Let's read a face

It's time we got a better idea of the many personality traits you'll be able to spot on anyone you see.

To the uninitiated, these photos are just of the faces of a woman and a man. But to the experienced face reader, especially someone who knows Psycho-Graphicology, these faces reveal much more. They're locked vaults to which we have the combinations.

Look at the photograph on the opposite page. Once you know Psycho-Graphicology, you'll know immediately that this smiling face belongs to a woman who is very comfortable around other people and accepting of who they are, as well as being vivacious. You'll also know that, as fun as she appears, she has a difficult time getting close.

What features stand out as you study her face? The most

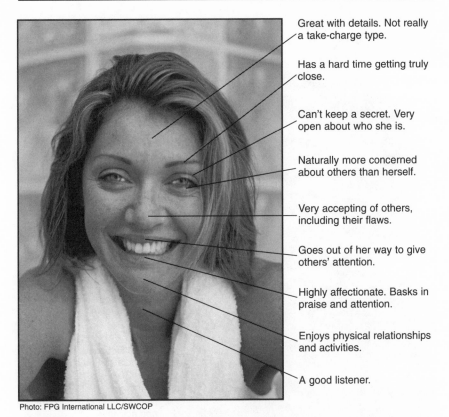

Great with details. Not really a take-charge type.

Has a hard time getting truly close.

Can't keep a secret. Very open about who she is.

Naturally more concerned about others than herself.

Very accepting of others, including their flaws.

Goes out of her way to give others' attention.

Highly affectionate. Basks in praise and attention.

Enjoys physical relationships and activities.

A good listener.

Photo: FPG International LLC/SWCOP

obvious is probably the tip of her nose. Big and round, it's a certain sign that this woman is very accepting of others, with all their weaknesses and shortcomings. You'd find her very uncritical.

The skin above her eyes is fairly loose and fleshy. You'll learn shortly that this feature belongs to un-controlling people, individuals who are comfortable letting the world see who they really are and usually don't try to control others.

Now look at her lips. Even though she is smiling, it's easy to tell that her lips are relatively large and full. This is your signal that she is very affectionate and, by nature, relishes and even seeks out the attentions of others.

Look next at her eyebrows. These belong to people who keep their distance from others. As affectionate as our subject is, you'd find her difficult to get truly close to. Finally, look at the size of her chin. It tells you that, if she likes you, connecting on a physical level would be an important part of your relationship. If your chin is roughly the same size, you'd be a good match in this area.

Compare her face with this one...

Naturally takes charge when there's a need.

Highly controlled and disciplined. An actor, he is good at hiding behind a facade.

Only moderately concerned about others' needs.

A hero-type. Not concerned about his safety.

Critical of others (to help them improve).

Very affectionate, loves others' attention.

Needs physical relationships and activities.

Photo © David Katzenstein/CORBIS

If you were to become interested in this fellow, among other things you'd find him intelligent, attentive, a true perfectionist and someone who loves quality in everything he buys. On the other hand, you'd also find out he's very uncertain of his own ideas and that he tends to overspend his budget regularly. But we're getting ahead of ourselves.

Look at his face. What features stand out? His forehead is reasonably wide, so we know he's the kind of person who would want to dominate your relationship, especially when he wants something.

His upper eyelids are not especially rounded, your sign that he probably does not concern himself with other people. His lower eyelid is a certain sign he also cares little about his own needs. He probably works too hard, rushes around too often, frequently not getting enough rest or eating the right foods.

The tight eyelid folds also tell us he has an intense need for control. It's his nature to feel a strong, unrelenting need to control himself and direct others.

The size of his lips, thin upper and full lower, tell us two more key traits. First, he is not inclined to pay others huge amounts of attention. At the same time, he's looking for someone who will give him plenty of affection.

Finally, look at his chin. Its size, large in relation to the rest of his face, is a sure sign he needs and enjoys physical contact in everything from sports to relationships. If you started dating this fellow, you might expect some fairly overt physical overtures early on in the relationship.

As you've just seen, all the information we can glean from a face is right on its surface, in the lines and creases, indentations, distances from one point to another and the shapes and sizes of different features. There are many facets to be analyzed that in different combinations reveal hundreds of distinct personality characteristics. You are going to learn the most important, most telling facial indicators to help you assess the personality traits of others and to help you find or keep the right romantic partner for you.

In an ideal world, we hopefully wouldn't be analyzing our subjects from their pictures. We'd want to have them standing in front of us. Still, isn't it remarkable how many insights we've gained from photographs? Imagine how much more you will learn when you are face to face with the object of your attraction.

What You'll See (and Not See) in His or Her Face

Psycho-Graphicology has nothing to do with reading someone's gestures, general appearance, body shape or body language. It's not about studying the bumps on the top of the head (called phrenology). It's also not about predicting the future.

Instead, this face reading method uncovers individuals' core needs and drives and a full spectrum of habits, likes, abilities, beliefs, attitudes, talents, tendencies, actions, expectations, limitations, thinking, preferences and tastes that come from these needs and drives. Whew! That's a lot of insider information that you will be able to digest and think about. But it will be very helpful as you make decisions about the romantic and perhaps marital suitability of the people you meet and date.

Let's be clear, however, about one thing: You won't be able to tell from reading his or her face if someone is capable of immoral, violent, dishonest or criminal behavior. The qualities that we can discern from face reading are substantial, but also somewhat neutral. These qualities indicate a person's natural tendencies or preferences, but not necessarily how the individual will choose to act on them. Psycho-Graphicology won't tell you if someone is of good character or bad; it won't tell you if someone has a dangerous or criminal side. What it will tell you is whether or not the new person in your life has personality traits that are similar or complementary to your own and, if so, how best to go about winning him or her over and building a mutually satisfying relationship. This method of face reading will also tell you, very quickly, who is not, and who may never, be right for you.

It is best to use face reading as your first—but not your only—indicator of what someone is like.

If you're thinking of spending a lot of time with this attractive new person in your life, use your common sense and intuition to get a better sense of what this individual is like. Don't walk blindly into a date or relationship just because his eyes look honest, his nose says he's not critical, his neck says he's a good listener or because you think he has a sweet, caring face.

As valuable and accurate as Psycho-Graphicology is, I recommend you don't use it solely on its own to evaluate a potential mate or even a date. Think of it as a potent and valuable tool. Use it in conjunction with your good judgment, experience and intuition, to initiate and build successful relationships and to zero in on people who will make the best spouse, lover or friend for you.

How you can use face reading to improve your relationship odds
You'll find many ways of using your new face reading knowledge to improve your chances of discovering the right partner for you. Read faces to be able to spot your future mate, agreeable new friends or people who have traits you value in others. When you know what those personality traits look like on the face, it's easy to find people who match what you want!

Use face reading as a way to get to know new acquaintances better. With this skill, you can peer inside everyone you meet. You'll be able to assess whether they'll be easy to talk to, to work with and to get to know. That's worth knowing early on!

Once you know what your current friends and partners are like, you can use the insights you get from face reading to guide your interactions with them. For example, in your relationships you might concentrate on what you now know is important to them or on things you both enjoy. Conversely, you may choose to shy away from areas where you aren't a good match with a particular individual.

Finally, as you use it more and more often, you will find that face reading gives you insights into virtually everyone you meet. As it has for me and my students, you will probably find that it helps you see beyond what people look like and helps you focus on what's more important—what they are really like inside, their inner core. No longer is that person just another stranger or clerk or bus driver or waitperson. Instead of seeing them as anonymous people, you will find that you are much more aware of them as individuals. Once you've read their faces, you'll probably find yourself much more accepting of people and how they think, act and talk. Suddenly, they are fellow human beings, with their own set of needs, drives, abilities and proclivities that aren't so different from yours.

You may discover that once you know how to read faces, you will recognize at a glance the people with whom you can connect and enjoy fruitful relationships. In the past, you may have overlooked potential partners or just assumed they would not interest you. Most every face will intrigue you now, because you'll be able to uncover the marvelous individuality and spirit hidden behind even the plainest, most ordinary faces.

The pitfalls of face reading and how to avoid them

It's unrealistic to say that you or I will always be completely, 100 percent accurate in our analyses. We won't. Many factors can come into play that affect your subjects' personalities and facial features and undermine accurate analyses.

Why? Not all faces are easy to read accurately. For example, you may not be able to tell if someone has had reconstructive surgery, such as a face-lift or nose job. Maybe they've plucked their eyebrows or they broke their nose. These details are important to know, if you can find out.

A smile can throw off your analysis, too. Have you noticed how a smile can change how an individual looks? As a face reader, you'll have to be especially careful of even slight smiles, since they can easily change the shape of the eyes, the mouth, the cheeks, the chin and even the nose. Your reading will be far more accurate when your subject's face is at rest, not smiling, not tense.

Occasionally, you'll find another challenge: Many folks, especially young people and highly self-controlled people, just don't know themselves very well. That won't necessarily make your analysis wrong. However, if you ask them to confirm what their faces are telling you, these people will often disagree. Don't let it throw you. Instead, relax, take a breath and know that you're probably pretty accurate in your assessment. Here again, trust the face to reveal personal characteristics and then back it up with your experience and intuition, which will grow along with your skill, over time.

Your face reading subjects may also disagree with you about who they are and what they are like if they have decided to live their lives in ways that are out of sync with their true personalities. As you'll discover, some people do live at odds with their true selves. For example, there is no way you can know by looking at someone's face that he had an experience that affected him greatly and profoundly changed how he conducts his life. Perhaps, because of her upbringing, a woman may have consciously or unconsciously changed, controlled or modified her behavior and thinking. In fact, some people may have completely overridden key portions of their natural personalities.

You may also get disagreement from people who were brought up by parents who guided them to act and live a certain way, possibly according to rigid standards. Or perhaps they grew up under the influence of a religion or culture in which certain types of thinking and behavior were encouraged and expected while others were discouraged and repressed. The innate characteristics of such people may be so deeply hidden they will never be allowed to emerge or be acknowledged.

When you analyze people like this—and often they will seem pleased to tell you that you're wrong—don't lose confidence in your abilities. Chances are, you're getting a pretty accurate picture of the 'real' person standing before you and they are leading lives that aren't reflecting their true personalities.

Of course, on rare occasions, your analysis of a particular facial feature may simply be wrong. It happens to all of us. After all, no one's perfect. People's faces can change almost moment-to-moment depending on what they're doing. Expressions can come and go and smiling or squinting can change features dramatically, making them impossible to read accurately. (Just try to read a chin or lips when your subject is talking or try to read their eyes when they are smiling.)

As you get better and better at face reading, your accuracy will climb to 80-90 percent or higher. You'll be correct just about every time. If you follow the methods and suggestions in this book and especially if you trust yourself and the Psycho-Graphicology method, you will become a skilled and successful face reader.

How to analyze that special someone

Once you learn the meaning of just a few facial features, you'll be eager to start applying your knowledge. Imagine yourself walking into a room and there before you are several unsuspecting attractive people just waiting to be analyzed. How do you proceed?

First, always do your analysis when your subject is at ease. Otherwise you'll find many facial features will read inaccurately. Pay particular attention to the person's eyes, mouth and cheeks. Are these features relaxed? They're probably slightly or significantly contorted if the person is talking, smiling or exhibiting some other facial expression.

Once you catch the face at rest, you can approach your face analysis in two ways. Chances are, you'll end up using both methods, depending on your circumstances.

Using the first method, you seek out and "read" specific facial features, looking for particular personality traits. You might use this technique if you're looking specifically for a person with a strong sex drive, a very affectionate nature or some other clearly defined trait you seek in a partner or spouse. When you discover the specific trait you're looking for, don't stop your analysis. I *strongly* recommend you proceed to study the rest of his or her face. Don't assume that simply because the person has one trait you are looking for that the two of you will make a great or even a good couple! You need to look at the entire package.

In the second approach, instead of zeroing in on a pre-selected feature or set of traits, you scan the person's entire face, looking for elements that just seem to jump out at you. What features get your attention either because they're proportionately a little too large or too small for the face? I've found that such features often signify many of the person's most illuminating personality traits and many of their dominant tendencies. And because they are probably predominant traits, you'll want to know about them right from the beginning of your relationship.

There is a third approach: You measure each facial feature. While measurement can be useful, I've found it's not necessary and simply too impractical for most situations. Usually, a feature's *relative* size—its size compared with the rest of the face—will be all you'll need to get an accurate assessment.

A final word of warning: Remember that in a relationship with another person, you're getting the whole package. You're going to have to deal with all the personality facets that his or her face is telling you about. Don't succumb to the easy temptation to ignore or minimize unattractive traits you may not like just because you've found other traits that you do like. Sure, finding someone who likes a strong physical relationship, as you do, is great, but is it really worth it when that same person has a neck that, like a flashing neon sign, broadcasts his tendency to be very stubborn and a poor listener? Consider *everything* the face tells you before you decide if he or she is the one for you.

How to learn the facets and become comfortable with reading faces
You can bring the information in this book to life and quickly make it the helpful tool it's meant to be if you'll do more than just read through these pages.

In my classes, some of my students report being a bit over-whelmed by face reading at first, mostly because it's new to them. I admit it seems like a lot to attempt. First, you have to get used to examining faces for their information value. Next, you must train yourself to look at specific features and remember what they mean. Then you assess their relative size and, finally, you come to conclusions.

At first, it's a lot to remember. But, like my students, in a short time you'll find it coming together very quickly. You'll become comfortable and adept. It'll be second nature to look at a pointed nose tip and say to yourself, *Boy, is that guy critical!*

Again, practice is imperative. Just keep doing it. Most of us see so many people in a day that if you learned just one new trait a day and watched intently for it for the next twenty-four hours, you'd know it cold and remember it forever. In fact, with daily practice, you could master everything in this book in twelve days or less!

As you read each section on individual facial features, you'll be amazed at how much better you will be able to learn and remember this information if you can associate each facial feature and personality trait with people you know. For example, instead of trying to remember that a pointed nose indicates a critical person, remember that Uncle Ed has a pointed nose and, boy, can he be critical!

As you're reading, take a moment to put the book down and think of friends, family members, old lovers, partners, colleagues and others who have this particular feature. Who has the pouty lower lip you're reading about? Who has the thick neck? The very rounded eyes?

When you see again and again that people you know have a certain facial feature and the personality trait that goes with it, you'll prove to yourself the accuracy and value of Psycho-Graphicology and you'll become even more inspired to use it often.

Keep a mirror near your book as you're reading. You'll want to look at your own face from time to time to analyze your own personality. Not only will this help you remember what you're reading about, but when you see similar or completely different features on someone, you'll also be able to assess with greater accuracy how compatible the two of you will be.

I also suggest that you gather together photographs of family and friends and start analyzing them. Get pictures of your parents and siblings, too. You'll be amazed at what you'll see in their faces and it may explain a lot about how they acted toward you when you were growing up. Look through your high school or college yearbooks and see what you can read in your old friends' and schoolmates' faces. (This may prove more challenging since these pictures may not only be retouched, but our faces are often not as well-defined in our younger years as they are when we are older.)

Look at your boss. Look at your coworkers. Go visit your neighbors. (But don't tell them what you're doing, yet.) Pick up a copy of your favorite celebrity magazine and look at the pictures. Check out our government leaders. Watch television just for the fun of analyzing the actors, newscasters and other personalities. From now on, when you watch the *Tonight Show* and notice Jay Leno's prominent chin, you'll enjoy knowing what it says about Jay.

Above all, as is often said, practice, practice, practice. It's really lots of fun and there are plenty of opportunities. After all, there's a face for every person in your life. And those faces will give you valuable information about why people do what they do and say what they say... and why one individual may be the romantic partner of your dreams and someone else may be the nightmare.

Two reasons why face reading works

In the nearly three decades that I've been reading faces, I have found two sound explanations why face reading works. One is scientific, one more metaphysical.

You have probably noticed how people who seem to have difficult lives also seem to have faces that look older, more haggard. Why is that? Science itself has recognized a strong relationship between our experiences and our face structure. The relationship: Our emotional and psychic experiences lead to the development of certain muscles and the production of specific hormones that, in turn, directly influence the size and shape of our facial features.

As Dr. Leopold Bellak and Samm Sinclair Baker, co-authors of *Reading Faces* (Holt, Rinehart and Winston, 1981) and avid students of the human face, write:

> *Innate characteristics and life experiences not only leave their marks on the surface of the skin but also influence the contours of the muscles and bone structure beneath. As a matter of fact, it is the habitual*

pull of these muscles of facial expression on both the skin above and the bones below which, to a large extent, determine facial characteristics.

Dr. Bellak and Mr. Baker also note that testosterone, a hormone that both men and women produce, has a profound effect on both bone structure and muscles.

In short, when we habitually act a certain way (such as repeatedly displaying certain facial expressions) our bodies respond by producing certain hormones and by building muscles under the skin that help give our faces their shape. These hormones and muscles actually modify or shift our facial structures so that our faces can end up being close reflections of our lives.

Face reading works for a second, more abstract reason, too. I believe that when we read a person's face, we are also intuitively sensing and interpreting the energy that makes up and surrounds the human body. Just like everything else, the human body is fundamentally energy, a massive, ingenious conglomeration of molecules. Our bodies are also surrounded by electromagnetic fields that people sensitive enough to read subtle human energy patterns call our auras. Just as we use our five senses to hear, see, smell, touch and taste the world around us, I believe that at the same time we are using our skill to read faces, we also use our intuition, our sixth sense, to 'read' this energy. Most people don't realize we humans have this ability, yet we use it all the time when we assess people we have just met.

Psycho-Graphicology is a way to relate specific facial characteristics to different, subtle types of energy that we sense and interpret. In other words, if you'll forgive the pun, we're able to put a 'face' on our intuitive insights.

If understanding why it works will help you trust in the value and accuracy of reading faces, then use it. But it really makes no difference whether you believe the scientific, physical explanation, the energy-based metaphysical explanation or both. You'll find Psycho-Graphicology just plain works and as soon as someone whose face you're reading drops their jaw, looks you right in the eye and exclaims, "Wow! How did you know that?" you won't care why!

Two rules for the face reader to remember

If you've begun reading faces already, you've discovered that facial features and personality traits exist at many levels between high-level and low-level traits described and pictured in this book. You may even have noticed that traits at the same level may look different from person to person depending on their age, their race and even their gender.

So how do you account for things like age, gender or race when you read faces? It's easy when you remember two simple "rules":

Rule #1

The Rule of Proportion:

Compare a feature's size with the entire face and the rest of the features

The first important key to successfully reading faces is: always compare each facial feature with the rest of the features. Ask yourself, *Is this feature proportionate to the rest of the face? How does it "fit" this face?*

Be sure you look at relative feature size, *not* just absolute feature size. It's not as important whether the distance from A to B is, say, one inch. What is important is if the distance makes that feature more prominent or less prominent when compared with other features on the person's face. For example, let's say a subject's nose is very wide at the bottom, yet it's *not* large compared to many other features such as the lips or eyes. In that case, we would "read" it as average size, probably not large.

Said another way, if the feature fits the general size and shape of the face, it's probably a facet of moderate importance in the person's life. If it appears disproportionately large or small for the face, that's your signal that, if large, it might be a high-level facet that strongly influences the individual's thinking, drives and behaviors or, if small, a low-level facet with little or no influence on his or her personality.

Reading men, reading women

You've probably noticed that men tend to have larger heads than women. Should you take that into account in your analysis?

As you now know from Rule #1, the Rule of Proportion, at this point it makes little difference in your analysis how large a person's head is. We're only concerned about *relative* size, not precise measurements.

If you see a nose that looks quite wide on a woman with a small head and petite features, it will have a much greater significance than if this same-sized nose belonged to a man with a large head and face.

I recall seeing a photograph of two company presidents side by side. One was a man with a wide forehead; one was a woman with a smaller head and a somewhat narrower forehead than the man. Yet both had the exact same drive and ability to successfully manage businesses and this is evidenced by the fact that both foreheads were *proportionately* the same size.

At first glance, this method of face reading may appear to work best on certain people with certain characteristics. However, I can assure you that with practice you can use it with tremendous accuracy on just about anyone.

You may also have noticed that different races and ethnic groups have differing features. This will present no problem for you as you read people's faces if you always remember Rule #1 and the following rule.

And that leads to our next guideline:

Rule #2

The Rule of Relativity:

Feature size is relative to the subject's race, ethnicity or gender

You need to consider Rule #2 when you read faces because, once again, everything is relative.

In your analysis, always observe how the facial feature compares to the rest of the subject's face and to other faces you've seen that belong to other members of your subject's ethnic background, race or gender.

In your analysis, ask yourself: *Compared to other members of this person's race, ethnic group or gender, is this feature large or small? Prominent or not? Does the feature dominate the face relative to the other features? Does the feature fit the face or is it relatively large or small?*

The truth is, if you're reading faces correctly, you're not going to be seeing each race or ethnicity as having the same facial features. Instead, you'll see one individual at a time. You'll see a group of *individuals*, each person with his or her own unique combination of facial features and personality facets.

That's the beauty of this method. Once you stand face to face with a man or woman of any race or ethnicity and start looking at their features, their gender and race virtually disappear. Stereotypes vanish and you see before you a person with a unique combination of individual features, a singular being with his or her own set of talents and abilities, needs and tendencies.

You're going to realize very quickly that every person you study looks different—not the same—and you'll come to identify and appreciate the differences.

You'll be able to read anyone's face accurately—men and women of any race or ethnic background—as long as you remain aware of Rules One and Two and concentrate on the relativity and proportion of the person's facial features.

"But he doesn't act the way his face says he should!"

If his facial features say one thing, but his behavior and his words say another, think twice (or three or four times) before assuming your analysis is wrong. He may be putting on a great show. Given time, his true personality will emerge.

Time will reveal that your partner's face really is an accurate road map to his or her personality. So use it. Study it. Compare the way he presents himself with what his face says.

One of my students, Ted, was clearly talented at attracting women. He was so polished, so caring and interesting that women flocked to him. These women saw him as a wonderful, affectionate guy. Of course they did, because they evaluated their relationships the old-fashioned way: The women judged him by his actions and his words. No, no, no! Wrong, wrong, wrong!

Had his girlfriends been able to read his face, they would have known that Ted's persona was all an act, a mere facade. When I first saw him (before I learned of his lady-killer reputation), I could see that he was a consummate actor. Underneath the warm, charming exterior was a man who really cared only about himself, easily found fault with others and really wanted only one thing from women—sex. It took weeks or even months for most of his girlfriends to uncover the true Ted, recognize their incompatibility and then suffer the emotional pains of ending their relationships.

The same was true of one of my female friends. Like Ted, Karen attracted men like honey attracts bees. Besides being cute, she was very affectionate, thoroughly enjoying men's company. Unlike Ted, however, Karen was almost never interested in physical relationships. Instead, she liked men who were intelligent, men who put a premium on using and developing their minds. Her affectionate personality, however, seemed to attract men who were more physical in their approach to women and relationships and who misinterpreted her affectionate nature. These men were invariably shot down when they tried to push the physical side of the relationship too far.

Their misunderstanding of Karen's true personality made for a lot of dissatisfying relationships—on both sides. But there it was, written all over her face: "I value intelligence a lot more than sex." Too bad not one of these guys could see it until it was too late.

Will face reading tell me if we are compatible?
Will Psycho-Graphicology reveal if you and your potential partner are compatible? The simple answer is: Yes. It's of great value because it will show you specific areas in which you and he or she are well suited and will be more compatible with each other. On the other hand, face reading can also show you where you're not matched.

You're not going to find the whole answer to the question of compatibility in face reading. Compatibility is such a large, broad-ranging issue that facial features themselves cannot be considered a foolproof method of determining if a new acquaintance is the perfect partner or friend for you. If there is such a thing as complete compatibility (and I'm not sure there is), you'll only start to answer that question by carefully assessing every aspect of your individual lives and your relationship, including studying all the facets in both of your faces, noticing how each of you react to different experiences, trusting what your intuition tells you about each other and honestly assessing if this person truly makes you happy.

Think of reading faces as a tool—a very worthy tool. Use it to verify your observations, experiences and gut feelings about people. If you want to know if you're compatible with your partner, compare your facial features. But don't stop there. Keep asking yourself these tough, important questions: Do we share common interests? Are our goals similar? Is there a strong bond here? What values do we share? Try to be as honest as you can. And remember to be honest about assessing those areas where face reading has shown that you may be incompatible.

A quick tip on "trait compatibility": As a very general rule, if you're looking for a partner who is compatible with you in a particular area (such as touching, affection or compassion), look for facial features that are similar in shape or in size (proportionately) to yours. Are your chins equally "deep" in proportion to your faces? Do your lips complement his or hers? How about your eyes? The more these match up, the more compatible the relationship will be over the long term.

There are important exceptions to this rule of thumb. Some personality traits complement each other because they are opposites, not because they are the same. For example, an individual who loves to immerse herself in details would probably be more comfortable—in this area—with a partner who is the opposite, someone who loves to take charge and delegate the details.

So, if you're going to use Psycho-Graphicology to find friends and romantic partners who are good matches for you in specific areas, it's a good idea to first pay attention to who *you* are and what *you* need. Then watch for features on others that best match or complement you and your personality.

Split personalities:
Two eyes, two ears...our two-sided face
Have you ever noticed that the left side of a face is often slightly different than the right? If you haven't, take a closer look at your own face in a mirror. You may see one ear that sticks out a little

farther than the other. Or an eyelid that's longer than the other. Or one corner of the mouth that curves up while the other curves down.

Just how do you analyze that? First, recognize that there are two sides to every face. Your subject's left side (on the right as you look at them) is related to the right side of their brain, while their right side (on your left as you face them) is associated with the left side of their brain.

On most people, each side is *slightly* different. Perhaps four or five features out of the dozens we can study differ just a bit from side to side. Once in a while, you'll see a face with very distinct differences on the left and right sides. What does that mean? It may mean nothing, or you may find that this person will tend to be moody, perhaps even act somewhat unpredictably.

The important thing to remember is that when you're reading a face, check out both sides. When you see a facial feature that looks one way on one side and a different way on the other, know that your subject's personality actually changes from time to time reflecting both sides. To be accurate in your analysis, you'll want to take that into account.

This lesson hit home with me early on in my face reading career. Ken was a college friend of mine. One day I'd find Ken optimistic and excited about his life. I'd see him a few days later and he'd be depressed, pessimistic, expecting the worst from every situation. I wondered how he could be so distinctly different each time I saw him. When I asked him what was going on, he claimed nothing had happened that brought about the shift in his outlook and emotions. He said he just felt differently.

Years later, when I learned to read faces, I went back to Ken's yearbook picture and found the answer: One corner of his mouth curved up and the other curved down. Sometimes he was an optimist and sometimes a pessimist.

Over the years I've seen many other examples of such splits in personality and attitude. People complain to me about their spouses—sometimes they're really frisky and constantly wanting sex, while at other times they won't be physically affectionate for any reason. Others complain that their significant other suddenly shifts from being very involved in their relationship to acting disinterested.

Often the answer is right there on their faces—on the left and on the right. So watch both sides. If they don't match, you may learn something important.

How to Read Facial Features So You Can Assess That Special Person

Let me anticipate a question you may be asking: How can faces—something we all have, something that varies so much and looks so different from person to person—be accurately broken down into separate features that can be illustrated and described in this book of modest length?

That's a very good question and it offers me a platform to introduce the features themselves so that you can form the right impression of that man or woman you meet and find yourself attracted to.

Of course, the professional study of face reading is complicated and takes more time and effort than you probably want or can devote to it, especially if you are anxious to come to some immediate decision as to whether or not you want to pursue a relationship. To get you started quickly and easily, I'm going to show you twelve of the most important facial features and dominant personality traits associated with each one.

Also, for simplicity and ease of learning, instead of discussing each of the dozens of small variations you might see in each feature, we will confine our study to two extremes using illustrations of facial features. Then you will be able to study those features to see which extreme fits better.

These two extremes are termed "high-level" and "low-level." High-level personality traits are those that convey strong drives in the individual's life. They are intense needs that are difficult to ignore and often are accompanied by distinct talents and abilities. Low-level traits, on the other hand, are the exact opposite. When you spot a low-level facet, you're looking at a trait that has little or no significance in that person's life. In most cases, a person who displays a low-level trait has no need to achieve fulfillment, no drives and no associated talents or abilities in this particular area.

You're going to see how to spot the most controlling people and the least, the most compassionate and the least caring, the most touch-hungry and the least and so forth. These basics are the foundation you need to make face reading useful to you in a social context from this day forward.

When you start examining real faces, you'll see that there are many variations beyond the illustrations you'll see here and many levels in-between the two extremes we're showing you. But don't worry. When you know how to identify the two ends of the spectrum of a particular trait, you'll have the knowledge (and you'll soon have the confidence) you need to assess where almost anyone sits on the scale.

In the pages that follow, you'll find a list of personality traits associated with each feature. Of course, not everyone who sports a particular facial feature talked about here will have *all* the personality traits mentioned. However, you will find they will have *many* of them and they *always* have the fundamental need or drive that the feature indicates. As a general rule, the higher level (meaning "the stronger") the trait that person has, the more personality characteristics associated with it he or she will exhibit.

Interrelated Traits

Each individual facial feature we're about to study has a corresponding personality trait. Each trait influences its owner in two ways. First, the trait stands on its own directly affecting thinking, beliefs, attitudes and behavior. However, the effect doesn't stop there. In combination with other traits, it also influences and modulates other, sometimes seemingly unrelated, aspects of the man or woman's personality.

You'll be able to figure out what impact individual traits have on each other most of the time by using logic. For example, in your present dating situation, can you guess how a person with a high need for physical contact *plus* a high level of determination would act? Now compare that person with someone who has a high need for lots of physical contact, but lacks determination or is very self-controlled. The first person will probably be much more persistent or intent on establishing a physical connection than the latter individual, even though they both have the same need for touching and physical intimacy.

Don't jump to conclusions about someone after observing only one facial feature. Instead, get all the information you can and carefully fit together the pieces that form the bigger picture. Putting together the pieces of the *whole* personality and concluding how the different facets affect each other will create an accurate and fascinating picture of the person to whom you are attracted and will give you a much more realistic, comprehensive portrayal than assessing just one piece of the personality puzzle. Seeing the big picture will help you assess whether that special person you are studying is the right one for you.

THE FOREHEAD

How to tell whether that person to whom you are attracted wants to run your life:

The width of the upper forehead tells you how much a person needs to take charge.

Wide forehead—"I'm in charge here"

High-level—The wide front forehead

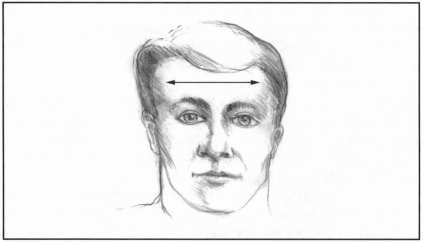

Practical and very much a "take-charge" person,
this wide-forehead individual loves to lead

Have you ever wondered what living with General George Patton or Genghis Khan would be like? If you link up with someone whose forehead looks as wide as the Goodyear Blimp, you'll find out. On a good day, you'll say Wide Forehead is fatherly (or motherly, if she's a woman), very helpful and reassuring. On a bad day, you'll say he or she dominates your relationship and you'll curse the person for being overbearing, bossy and even arrogant.

So which is it? Well, you'll discover it's all those things and more. Wide Foreheads love to be in charge; they NEED to be in charge. When they enter a room or situation, they just naturally take over and start managing everything.

Quick Tips

The width of the upper forehead tells you how much the person you are attracted to wants to manage you and almost everything and everyone in his world.

Highest Levels: The wider the upper forehead, the more she is driven to take over and run things.

Lowest Levels: When the upper forehead is narrow, he would just as soon let someone else take charge.

How to measure: Look at the highest part of the forehead (above the temples) when evaluating this trait. Observe the distance from one side to the other at the front of the head.

Want to turn your problems over to someone else to solve? How about turning your whole life over to someone else to manage? Wide Foreheads are up to the task and they'll love you for letting them! They think—without a doubt—that they know what's best for you, including how you should run your life. If you like being taken care of, you may find yourself attracted to the wide forehead, take-charge types. Most have an all-knowing, parental quality about them. They can have such a powerful presence that you could find yourself almost instinctively paying them surprising amounts of respect—the respect you usually reserve for your employer, a professor or some other authority figure.

Not that Wide Foreheads are necessarily asking for such deference. They often aren't. However, Wide Foreheads get respect anyway, because they often seem so darn sure of themselves.

The world is full of people with wide foreheads and, not surprisingly, they're often those who are put in charge. For example, look at the foreheads of people who run countries, head big corporations, command armies or lead social or political movements. Very often these movers and shakers have broad foreheads. Wide Foreheads are doers. They include hundreds of well-known people, including such diverse but powerful individuals as Richard Nixon, Disney boss Michael Eisner, former football coach John Madden, Martin Luther King, Winston Churchill, Gloria Steinem, Rosie O'Donnell, Bill Clinton, Al Capone, Larry King and many, many others.

A Wide Forehead is a true take-charge individual. Be warned: Even if you become his or her lifelong companion, you'll probably never be a full partner. Allowing others to contribute and forming final decisions together is not in this individual's nature.

> **A Key Facet**
>
> *Personality traits covered in this section are those of especially dominant personalities. At its highest level, the need to take charge, to organize and to manage is so powerful that it usually profoundly influences every aspect of such people's lives, careers, hobbies, love lives, parenting, friendships—everything.*

Despite the inability to form consensus either in private or work lives, why are people with broad foreheads so often high achieving and successful?

First, Wide Foreheads love to get things done—they *need* to accomplish. Add to that their love of jumping into the fray and taking charge. They want to run the show. And why not? These self-confident people also like to believe they know how to do everything. (To be fair, they often do know how; it's just that when they don't, they're not very good about admitting it.)

Wide Foreheads are naturally gifted at seeing "the big picture." Few things are more aggravating for them than having to get involved in the little stuff. They generally hate dealing with details and would much rather turn over the minutia, the trivia and the many particulars of daily life to someone else, so they can focus on the big issues.

You'll also discover that these men and women are very down to earth and highly practical. In just about every aspect of their lives, they are thinking, living and acting systematically. Everything is organized and in its proper place (including you).

You might disagree if you were to see a Wide Forehead's home or office. You may find stacks of papers, books, clothes, tools and laundry piled from one corner to another. Depending on your personality, you might call it messy or even chaotic. Not Wide Forehead. Ask him to find something specific for you and he will know right where to look. It may not appear to be, but his environment is totally organized. In the same way, a Wide Forehead will tend to compartmentalize his love life, keeping his emotions and emotional ties to his partner neat and organized.

Do our foreheads indicate we are a good match?
Men and women with wide foreheads naturally attract people who are willing to follow their leads, people who don't mind being overshadowed by them. As a general rule, such take-charge people do better with partners who sport narrower brows, people who enjoy handling the details with which Wide Foreheads can't be bothered.

Will you be content standing in the shadows? Really? This is one facial feature about which you'll want to be brutally honest in assessing. Do you sincerely enjoy take-charge people? Do you really like having others run the show? If so, you may find a relationship with Wide Forehead to be a comfortable fit for you, low-stress and low-exertion. If, however, you want an equal say in decisions and a pro-active role in the relationship, you had better think twice before opening your heart to an individual with a broad forehead.

Women and men with wide foreheads
Think of a man with a wide forehead. Now, think of a woman with a wide forehead. If you *don't* see them as equally wide, you're right. As a rule, women don't have foreheads as wide as men. In fact, a woman's forehead doesn't have to be as wide as a man's for her to be a brilliant manager, leader and take-charge person. Remember, the analysis of facial features, their size, placement and details, must be considered in terms of their relativity and proportion to the rest of the face and the size of the head as well as to which gender the subject belongs.

Their foreheads may not be as wide as a man's...

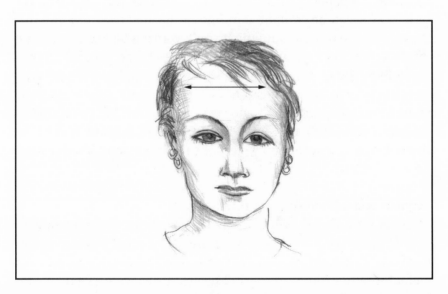

...but both of these women are real take-charge people.

Engaging the person with a wide forehead

Remember, these broad-browed individuals tend to be no-non-sense, take-charge people. They can be a bit brusque. Busy concentrating on the big picture, they also may not be interested in hearing everything you have to say, especially if your specialty is considering the details.

If you are attracted to a person with these traits and want to get his attention, here is the way to get started on the right foot. Since he understands and appreciates other strong, practical, take-charge people, your first job is to let him know you can be that way, too. Show him that you can be as powerful and in control as he is. Once you have his attention, however, back off a bit. After all, you don't want to enter into a competition with him (that's not very romantic and besides, you'll probably lose).

You'll gain Wide Forehead's respect if you show that you, too, can see and appreciate the big picture, the bigger issues. A few pointers when you're talking together: Get to the point quickly, sound as practical in your views as you can and don't question his need to be in charge or his belief that he knows best. If adopting these suggestions is not difficult for you, you may find that a relationship with a Wide Forehead can be safe, secure and loving.

The Narrow Forehead—In need of a manager!

Low-level—The narrow front forehead

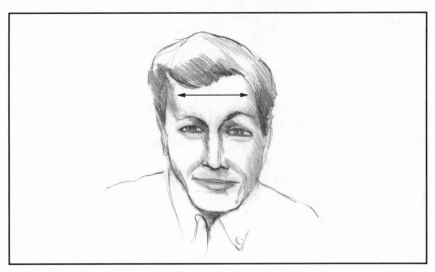

People with narrow foreheads are detail-oriented and full of ideas, but very willing to let others take the lead.

If Wide Forehead wants to run the world, you've probably already guessed what Narrow Forehead wants to do...anything but! This individual much prefers to let others take control of situations and lead.

Just as Wide Foreheads can't help but be practical, you'll probably find that Narrow Foreheads frequently are quite impractical. They can often become mired in the details and handle things at less than peak efficiency. While Wide Foreheads relish running things, their narrow counterparts usually don't want to be in charge. While Wides like to dominate you, you'll probably find that Narrows would simply prefer to be your friend.

Narrow Foreheads are often unassuming and, unless they also are very self-controlled, they are likely to be attracted to people who enjoy running things, such as Wide Foreheads.

Though opposites, the Wide and Narrow Forehead complement each other well. The two frequently make a great team. While the practical partner is very good at setting goals and laying out the grand scheme, the narrow partner thrives on exploring these goals and bringing the plan to fruition. Narrows take on the details that make successfully reaching bigger goals possible. Marriage or a romantic relationship between a Wide and a Narrow Forehead can be mutually beneficial, a true, symbiotic pairing.

Many Narrow Foreheads have another wonderful trait—they tend to see possibilities in everything, even the impossible. The problem is that, while they can envision the

> **Wide and Narrow:**
> **A great team**
>
> *If one of you has a wide forehead, the other's had better be narrow...or, at the very least, the other individual should be able to tolerate being told how to conduct his or her daily affairs. Narrows are frequently attracted to the strength and power of Wides, while Wides often benefit from Narrows' unassuming, more laid-back personalities.*

results they want, they don't always have a practical, down-to-earth understanding of how to get there or they are easily side-tracked. Again, this is another instance where a Wide Forehead partner could enhance a Narrow Forehead's life.

You'll quickly discover that, because she lacks practicality, the Narrow Forehead is lost in (and in love with) details. Forget seeing the forest. She sees only the trees...and the bushes...and every weed and blade of grass on the forest floor.

It's an unusual combination of traits in narrow-foreheaded people. On one hand, they can often come across as unrealistic, dreamers, perhaps a bit eccentric, even irrational. On the other hand, however, they also can be quite visionary. You'll probably find them to be highly imaginative and full of ideas and, unless they're severe pessimists, you'll also hear them tell you that nothing's impossible. When teamed up with the right wide-foreheaded partners for them, this is true.

Engaging the person with a narrow forehead

If your upper forehead is wider than the person's to whom you're attracted, you have two proven ways to engage him or her. First, just be yourself. As this individual comes to see you as someone who knows what you want, someone who knows how to get things done, she will feel right at home with you. In the meantime, while she is taking the time to get to know you, try this approach: Examine her face for other features that complement yours. Use these features as your starting point. Check out her chin (for touch) and her lips (for affection). If nothing strongly stands out, just ask her what she likes and get her talking. Allow yourself to delve into the details of a situation or a discussion with her. She'll feel comfortable and instantly connected with you.

THE EYEBROW

How to discover who wants
intimacy and commitment...and who doesn't:

Eyebrows tell just how involved—or
uninvolved—your potential partner will be.

The lofty eyebrow—Cool and distant

High-level—Elevated eyebrows

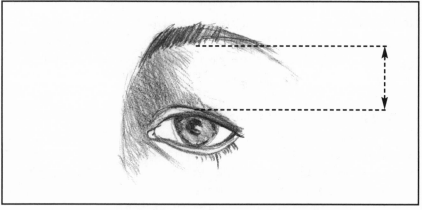

*Eyebrows that sit high above the eye at its
center indicate a person who has a hard
time becoming involved with others.*

Perhaps you have experienced this type of individual: You
go out together and have a great time. You're feeling very attracted
to her and want to get closer. You would like to take your relationship to the next level. You're also pretty sure she feels the
same way. Then you call, make a date and see her again. While
she's smiling and seemingly having a great time, you can't help
but sense a coolness, a distance between you two that you didn't
notice before. Suddenly, you find yourself wondering: *If she wants
a relationship, why is she so standoffish?*

People erect barriers and put space between themselves
and potential mates, lovers or friends for lots of emotional or

---

Quick Tips

The height of the eyebrows is an easy way to tell how involved a man or woman likes to get with the other people in his or her life.

Highest Levels: If the bottom edges of the eyebrows at their mid-points are considerable distances above the upper edges of the eyelids at their mid-points, your potential partner likes to keep herself at arm's length.

Lowest Levels: When the centers of the eyebrows rest close to the eyelids at their mid-points, your new friend will enjoy totally immersing himself in your life.

How to measure: From the centers of the eyebrows, assess the distances from the bottom edges of the eyebrows to the upper-most points of the eyelids over the centers of the eyes.

---

psychological reasons. Some people, however, just can't help it—it's innate. One of the first things you have to do in any new relationship is to check out his or her eyebrows.

Pick up a copy of your favorite magazine and you'll see pictures everywhere of people with elevated eyebrows. It's a look we frequently see on fashion models' faces today. Many celebrities, including Christina Aguilera, Brandy, Diana Ross, Luciano Pavarotti, Lucy Liu, Annie Potts, Annette Bening and others display high elevated eyebrows.

When you observe that your new romantic interest has eyebrows that sit high above each eye (measured right over the center of the eye), you know you've met someone who prefers to stay detached, someone who, by nature, keeps herself separate or distant from others.

The loftier the eyebrows, the harder you'll find it is to really get to know your new acquaintance. In fact, it could take years to get close enough to her that she'll feel comfortable lowering her protective barriers.

Highly elevated eyebrows indicate that an individual is most comfortable keeping virtually everyone—friends, lovers, family—at arm's length. Sure, he has relationships with people but he usually avoids becoming too immersed in them or very attached to anyone.

You can spot other outward signs of this trait quite easily. Watch the way he conducts himself. When you're talking with him, you'll probably sense an invisible emotional barrier between you. Instead of feeling a friendly connection or emotional "warmth," you may feel a subtle (or not-so-subtle) coolness or distance, almost as if he is pushing you away or keeping you outside a personal perimeter he has constructed. You may also notice a businesslike demeanor he displays toward people and situations. At the extreme, he may even act totally aloof. You may be surprised at how downright unfriendly he can appear to others.

Looking for an empathetic ear to whom you can tell your troubles? Sorry. You can't count on an understanding ear from this person. He has a hard time relating to others' problems. He may offer a shoulder to cry on, but he's just not good at empathizing.

Of course, this individual doesn't see himself as unfriendly, aloof or standoffish...and he can't understand why others might see him that way. In fact, dealing with a high-eyebrowed individual can be a bit confusing. On the one hand, you may be getting the message, "I'm interested in a relationship with you." At the same time, the person may be giving off cool, almost uninviting signals that leave you scratching your head. As a result, you are left feeling frustrated and probably wondering where to go with this relationship.

Do our eyebrows indicate we are a good match?
An important question is: How detached and independent are you? If your eyebrows rest high above your eyes like his or hers, then you may truly understand how this other individual feels and thinks. Possibly you feel comfortable with and tend toward "arms-length" relationships. If so, the two of you could be a very good match in this area.

On the other hand, if your eyebrows are low and hug your eyes, your needs in the critical areas of warmth and closeness are significantly different. You value and desire close, involved

When you see high-sitting eyebrows on that attractive new acquaintance, you also may notice an accompanying "arm's length" attitude. Before pursuing the relationship, think carefully about what levels of intimacy and emotion you require.

relationships. A person with elevated eyebrows will see you as much too eager to get involved, much too friendly and outgoing, and probably won't be comfortable with you. When your eyebrows and his or hers are this different, you should move cautiously in forming a relationship. If you were to marry or form a long-term committed union, you'll spend many hours wondering why your partner is holding back or if he or she is really committed to your relationship. You may find yourself worrying about what else you can do to make your loved one feel more connected, more intimately attached to you.

Engaging the person with high eyebrows

High Eyebrows are typically slow to make friends. Don't expect them to leap rashly into committed relationships. That's very unlikely to occur. They require the feeling of being independent, even at the expense of having close relationships, and they cherish their freedom and independence. If relationships are going to develop, chances are they will grow slowly at High Eyebrows' personal comfort levels and on their own terms.

Although it may be difficult to initiate and sustain a warm, close relationship with such an individual, you need to remember that this man or woman isn't all icy detachment. You must, however, approach him very slowly. Any relationship you might have with this sort of person will have to develop over time, the time it takes for him to allow you into his well-protected, inner emotional life.

Warning: Plucked eyebrows are deceiving.

If the object of your affection plucks her eyebrows, you're probably going to get a false reading in this area. Plucking changes the shape of the eyebrows. If you can, ask her if she plucks. Better yet, request a picture of her before she began to pluck her eyebrows.

Don't try to thrust yourself into his life. Don't try to get too close too soon. He's probably perfected methods of establishing barriers and he won't appreciate having you try to scale them right away. Let him suggest deepening and expanding the relationship. He most likely will be the one who sets the tone and pace for the closeness and intimacy of your commitment anyway.

If it's possible within your nature and if you really feel you want to, you also could start acting more like High Eyebrows. He'll feel more comfortable with your being a little more aloof than being overly intense. You could try acting a little less attentive and involved. Be a little distant, hold yourself at arm's length and appear preoccupied. When you converse with him, be objective and dispassionate about things. Like him, show you also can hold yourself apart and guard your independence.

What happens if he likes you and starts to open up a bit? You'll find he can occasionally warm up and show warmth and affection toward special people. For such an individual, however, this can feel risky, uncomfortable and unnatural. Once he's shown his feelings, he may seem ill at ease with them and try to minimize his emotions. He may even wonder to himself why he let himself get attached to you in the first place.

I don't want to make it seem as though high-browed people are unapproachable, because they're not. You'll find, depending on their other facial features, that they can have big hearts, be very gregarious, can attend to you with great devotion and can even have wonderful senses of humor. Also on the plus side, you can count on them to be good sources of rational, impersonal advice about how to handle your problems. You just can't expect much sustained emotional warmth to come with the package.

Remember that as much as you may like his other traits—even if he is caring and wonderful and attentive and funny from the moment he meets you—there will always be a certain distance, an emotional holding back with which you will have to contend.

> *If you really want to attract Lofty Brows, you could start acting more like him. But be warned: Even if you're successful at projecting cool detachment, if you have low, "hugging" brows, it can be an exhausting challenge, one that is difficult to sustain.*

The low eyebrow—Totally involved with others

Low-level—The Low Eyebrows

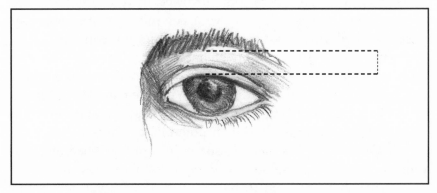

When the eyebrows are close to the eyes right
above their center, the person wants to be
totally involved in your life.

Do you want a partner who loves to get close, involved, totally immersed, completely attached, a person who lives for intimate, sustained relationships?

If you do, look for someone whose eyebrows sit right above the eyelids. This individual is Mr. or Ms. Involvement, a person who can't get close enough to you or involved enough in the things that interest him or her. Here's an individual who enthusiastically and single-mindedly throws herself into building and maintaining her relationships. That's the good news. The bad news is that she sometimes gets too totally committed and excessively involved in everything she cares about in her life: Her career, friends, relationships, pastimes, interests, everything. These close attachments with other people and her intimate involvement in every important aspect of her life make her feel happy and alive.

Close Eyebrows makes friends quickly and easily. She likes her relationships to be close and committed. Unlike her high eyebrowed counterpart, she lets herself get deeply attached to people. This is someone who has no difficulty committing to a long-term relationship and expects her partner to do the same.

Can you imagine dating or marrying someone who acts

just like you? It may sound odd, but men and woman with these low-slung eyebrows are able to identify so closely with people they like that they can take on their friends' or lovers' personality traits. As Low Eyebrows become involved in your life, they may become more like you, copying your common gestures, your pet phrases, displaying your sense of humor, your concerns, your goals and many other of your characteristics. These people can think and act so much like you that you'll probably find yourself feeling very comfortable with them. With their natural desire to establish a deep connection with others, it's no wonder they often seem to be an ideal match to their potential partners.

Close Eyebrows' need to sometimes plunge headlong into your life has a couple of serious drawbacks. First, you frequently can expect that her need to be so involved with you will mean she'll want to take center stage in your life. This may or may not work for you. Plus, over time her true personality will emerge—it has to—and will begin to overshadow this amazing persona that she has adopted and that you've come to enjoy so much. Your real relationship begins at this time.

Engaging the person with low eyebrows

The easiest way to engage Close Eyebrows is to be friendly, warm and welcoming to him. Act as if you already have a good relationship and presto, watch one appear! Talk to him about how much you value close associations, how you throw yourself into your work and into everything you do. Tell him about one of your problems. While Close Eyebrows may not be good at solving it for you (he can be so close and feel so attached to you that he has no objectivity), he will bask in the glow of being invited into your personal life and love the fact that you asked for his assistance.

If you're pretty sure he's attracted to you and is interested in a relationship with you (and if you want to deepen your connection), begin to introduce him to new, more intimate aspects of your life. Show him your photo albums. Invite him to dinner at your place. Have him meet you where you work one afternoon. Introduce him to your friends. Since he loves being involved in the activities and the lives of people he cares about, the more of yourself that you reveal and share, the more you'll appeal to his need to be involved...and the happier he will be in the relationship.

Will *you* be happy in such a close relationship? You now know how to find out...check *your* eyebrows.

Their level of involvement can vary
You can tell even more about the need of that special person in your life to involve or detach himself from others by looking at the height of the eyebrow as it approaches the side of the head.

This person will grow more distant...

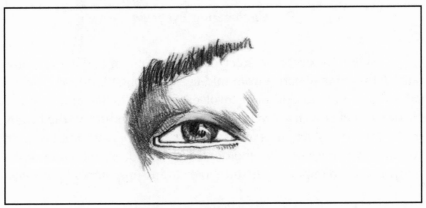

The Ascending Eyebrow

When you see eyebrows that move away from the eyes as they go out to the side of the face, usually getting higher as the brow extends, it is likely that over time this person will become more distant and less involved in his or her relationships. In other words, he may start by being totally involved and committed to the relationship (depending on the height of the brow over the eye's mid-point), but as weeks, months or years pass, this individual will gradually grow more distant. One day you'll notice that you and your partner are not enjoying the warm, close relationship you used to have. Instead of finding deeper meaning and comfort with his partner as time passes, this person becomes less interested, less engaged. If you choose to enter into a long-term commitment with someone who shows this trait, being forewarned may enable you to do something to change his tendencies or, at the very least, may lessen your future dismay and heartache.

This person's involvement will never change...

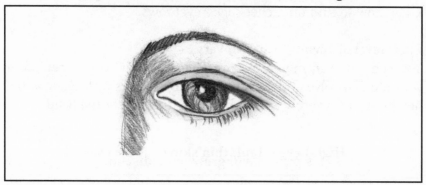

The Unchanging Eyebrow

When the eyebrows track close to the curve of the eye, maintaining the same distance from mid-eye to its outside corner, it indicates a person whose level of involvement won't change over time. He or she will be as involved or uninvolved, depending on the height of the eyebrows over the eyelids, in five years as five minutes after you met. For those of you who don't like surprises and value continuity, this is an important feature to examine on potential partners.

This person will become more attached...

The Descending Eyebrow

When you see eyebrows grow closer to the eyes as they move toward the side of the head—"closing in," so to speak—you know that this person's need to involve himself will increase over time. If you share the same need for close, enduring relationships, you're a good match.

SKIN ABOVE THE EYELID

How to learn if the new person in your life is a control freak:

Eyelids reveal those who need high levels
of control and those who don't.

The taut eyelid: A control freak

High-Level—Taut, thin skin over the eye

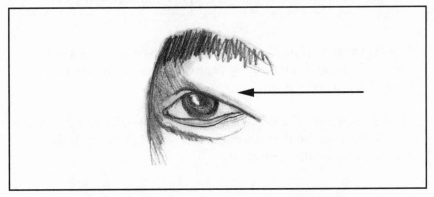

*Straight, tightly-pulled skin over the eyelid indicates
a person who needs to control others.*

Jealous. Secretive. Cautious. Possessive. Controlling. Manipulative. Poised. Image-driven. These are just some of the things you might say about a woman or man with high control needs.

When you look at the eyes of such individuals, you will probably see taut, thin skin that appears to be stretched across the corner of the upper eyelid on a downward slant, giving it a well-defined, sharp edge. When you see this facial trait you know you're in the presence of a highly controlling man or woman who wants (and needs) to control everything in life. Before becoming involved, you have to ask yourself an important question: How will you respond to someone with the compulsion to control you and your relationship? Only you can decide if a high-control person will make a good partner.

Quick Tips

The skin over the eyelids tells you whether your partner wants to control every facet of your life or is content to let you do what you please.

Highest Levels: When the skin over the eyelids (below the eyebrows) as it approaches the side of the face is pulled tightly so it has a well-defined "edge" to it and the skin appears thin, this person is both controlling of others and very self-controlled.

Lowest Levels: When the skin above the eyelids in the same area is fleshy and relaxed, the person lacks a strong need to control and is very open.

How to measure: The thinner and tighter the skin over the outside of the eyes (so that it usually hides part of the eye), the higher the need for control.

Are you ready to pursue or be pursued by someone who puts a premium on directing every facet of her life from the moment she hops out of bed in the morning until she drops off to sleep at night? Make no mistake...a high-control person wants every day of her life to go her way, according to her design. She wants to choose everything she does, often regardless of what you or anyone else (including her family and friends) wants. Plus, she goes to great lengths to ensure that events go the way she plans them.

As the name suggests, you'll find that high-control men and women love to set the guidelines in their relationships. Even if they have narrow foreheads, which often indicate less dominant personalities, High-level Controllers need to feel in charge. When they also have wide foreheads, indicating that they are take-charge people, these high-control people are even more demonstrative when wielding power, being the boss, giving directions, taking the lead and dictating who does what. Can you guess how they feel about other people telling them what to do?

One of your greatest challenges in a relationship with this man or woman will be getting to know him or her. It could take you a lifetime. Some people might even say it can't be done. Why? Because in addition to wanting to control their surroundings, people with this trait have a strong need to control themselves. High-control people make good actors. No, they're more than good actors, they are supreme actors, true masters of the craft. Start watching movies and studying photos of your favorite stars and look for the telltale tight eyebrow skin. You'll see that many fine Hollywood entertainers share this need for control and they're not alone. Many top politicians, super-salespersons and senior business executives are high-control people. This quality is a real asset for individuals who face tremendous pressure, yet need to appear calm and unflappable in public.

> **Reminder:**
> **Analyze the face only when your subject is at rest.**
>
> *If your partner is smiling or frowning at you, don't check for compassion, control, sexual appetite or any other personality trait seen in the eyes, cheeks, chin or nose just yet. Wait until the person is relaxed and his or her facial muscles are at ease. You'll get a much more accurate reading.*

Here's a challenge—try to recognize High-level Controllers by their behavior. That's a hard one! High-control people frequently don't seem to be controlling—at first. On the surface, they usually appear very poised, subdued and mild mannered. That may, however, be a facade. Inside, behind that even-keeled, calm exterior, their emotions can be running wild. So good are they at "acting the part" that their lives could be in total disarray and you'd never know it from their appearances or their interactions with others.

When you get to know them better, you will notice that they can be very calm for long periods of time and then suddenly, almost instantaneously erupt, displaying an intense and fierce wealth of emotions you would never have imagined possible from such buttoned-down people. Where did it come from? These individuals can only contain their emotional firestorms behind a relaxed-appearing, controlled surface for so long. Then they explode in all directions like volcanoes erupting.

Can you think of someone who has this tightly pulled skin cutting across their eyes? They are easy to spot when you know what you're looking for. You'll see high control on former Presidents Ronald Reagan and Dwight D. Eisenhower, Marlon Brando, Russell Crowe, Antonio Banderas, Brad Pitt, Jack Nicholson and Tom Brokaw. Take a look at their eyes. You'll find one of two types of skin above the eyes. On many, the skin is pulled tightly across the eye, concealing most or all of the eyelids. However, on people who have very rounded eyes (and eyelids), the skin may not be pulled over the corners of the eyes. On these individuals, you'll have to look carefully at the area where the upper edges of the eyelids and the lower edges of the skin above the eyes meet. The lines formed by these junctures are both very clearly defined *and* thin on high-control individuals and may appear almost razor-sharp.

> **The Compulsion to Control: Can you live with it?**
>
> *The need for self-control and control of others directly affect virtually every aspect of these people's lives. High-control individuals rarely let their guards down. They have a very difficult time relinquishing control of situations or tasks to others. They even sometimes struggle with knowing what is real and what is their self-constructed reality.*

Recognizing when a person, especially a favorite friend or romantic partner, has a need for high control can be more difficult than spotting other traits, but it is very important since this personality trait colors every aspect of his or her life. You might have a new friend or acquaintance who has a tremendous need to touch and be touched or is very affectionate. If he also needs to exert high levels of control, you probably won't be immediately aware of it, because he can be so good at concealing his true compulsions and desires.

High-Level—Curved eyelid with a sharp edge

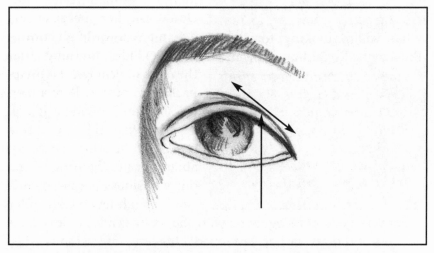

Sometimes you'll see high control in a curving eyelid.
Watch for the razor-sharp edge, a telltale sign.

The super control type is highly disciplined, which is an admirable trait. Firmly convinced he can be whatever he chooses, he finds himself driven to master his environment and himself. It's a belief that is both a curse (because he is sometimes frustrated in his efforts) and a blessing (because he is actually able to grow, change and often succeed). His love of discipline means he probably has interests and hobbies that revolve around self-control. He may enjoy the martial arts or embark on a rigorous mission of self-improvement. At the very least, he probably has a bookcase filled with self-help books or a history of taking self-help courses. You can find high-control people very attractive, because their discipline frequently helps them become successful

> **Is there a storm raging behind the calm exterior of the special person in your life?**
>
> *You might be surprised at the emotional upheaval that goes on beneath this individual's composed exterior. A model of poise on the outside, High-level Controller can be in turmoil on the inside. Since even a disciplined High-level Controller cannot hold everything inside all the time, however, eventually something "gives" and you'll get a rare peak into this most private soul.*

and powerful. Success and power, as has long been noted, are two of the greatest aphrodisiacs.

Behind the cool exterior, what is this high-control man or woman *really* like? Don't ask her, because she doesn't know. High-control people hide anything that they consider might be unappealing to others. Remember, for such an individual it's all about *acting* the part. She tends to be very secretive about her life, figuring it's no one's business but her own.

High-level Controller is not very good at recognizing who she really is and, unless she's had lots of therapy or has developed a life-long interest in self-discovery, she may even have convinced herself that she's someone she's not. This individual can be so caught up in her carefully created image, it's possible that she is living in a fantasy world, populated by people and events as she would like them to be, not as they truly are, herself included.

Not surprisingly, her need to control, manipulate or at least influence others can lead her into trouble. You may quickly discover that she enjoys suggesting what you should do and how to do it. She may feel the need to help you plan out your schedule or decide for you where to go for dinner or how to handle a difficult friend or career problem. Since high-control people can be very possessive, even jealous, she also may offer rather insistent suggestions about whom you should be friends with, whom you can trust, what you should do with the rest of your life and anything else that may have an impact on the relationship you share.

When a high-control person likes you, yet feels insecure about your liking them, he can spend endless hours thinking of ways to manipulate you to do what he wants and bring you under his wing. He may want to make you feel dependent on him. If you're sensitive to his manipulation and game-playing, very often you'll get the feeling that the High-level Controller is trying to make you one of his possessions. Of course, you'll need to tell him you disapprove. But if you do care about him, be careful how you express your displeasure. If you're indelicate, he may shut you out, purely in self-defense.

Control games

Highly controlled people have a tendency to employ little games to manipulate others when they're feeling insecure. When you're with a high control individual, be prepared to be "played" and practice saying "No."

A polished, secure High-level Controller will usually be more subtle in her attempts to engineer your behavior. Watch for little games she plays, especially comments and actions that are designed to get you to rely more on her, to trust her or to respond to her more positively. If she's like most high-control types, she's thinking of ways to get you to do what she wants. She just can't help it.

How to tell if your control levels match

With High-level Controller's ability to "act the part" and to shield things from you and himself, the high-control individual is often not well grounded in reality. What he needs is someone who is more reality-based, someone with a lower need for control and a higher need for truth, as well as a great deal more self-awareness. A partner with needs like High-level Controller's will most likely compete to be in charge and do nothing to help ground the relationship in reality. A relationship between two High-level Controllers will probably not be an easy alliance.

If my marriage is any example (I exhibit high control, my wife Pam shows none), a High-level Controller should make the effort to find a lower control mate or partner. I enjoy my privacy and the idea of controlling the world around me, while Pam wants direct communication, everything in the open and the same influence in our marriage as I have. It's an arrangement that can be especially challenging for me (given my need for control). Still, the combination of a High-level and a Low-level Controller has also proved very healthy for our relationship.

Engaging the High-level Controller

You've met her, you're attracted to her and now you want to get High-level Controller's attention. But how? Easy. First, you'll have to act reserved, restrained. After all, that's how she'll be acting and what she understands. Tell her less about yourself than you usually would. Be secretive and even a little mysterious. Remember, she loves secrets.

> **Peering behind the mask of a high-control partner**
>
> *Your opportunities to see the real person behind the facade will be few and far between. Since High-level Controller seldom really lets down her guard, you'll probably have to wait until a time when she is truly happy, secure and carefree... perhaps after you've shared a bottle of wine and she is feeling relaxed and at ease.*

If you can draw her out, you might be able to establish a close relationship quickly. One way to do that is to get her talking about herself, something she may not feel comfortable doing. Get her to share some secrets with you in a game of "You tell me about you, I'll tell you about me." You may not learn much at first, but you'll be helping her do something she may find surprisingly enjoyable—getting out of her shell and connecting at a deeper level.

Keep your expectations in check though. You're never going to learn everything about her. Ever. She likes her image and wants to maintain her well-practiced facade. Don't expect her to suddenly burst forth and reveal all her little secrets.

If you expect to see her emotional side, you may have to

wait...and wait...for that too. High-level Controller usually won't show you any strong sign of passion or give you a glimpse of her emotional interior unless she's concealing some very powerful, unsuppressible emotions. If you are patient and hang in there, the day will eventually come when she's hurting so badly that she can't hide her emotional upset any longer and she must share it with someone. That's when the authentic person and her passions will be revealed. These are special, rare times and if you're the person she chooses to open up to, they are also wonderful opportunities to grow closer.

Holding onto the High-level Controller

They hate surprises, so make sure your high-control man or woman always feels in control as much as possible, even if he or she is not. If you desire a long-term relationship with this individual, you'll want to continue to be mysterious, revealing yourself just a little at a time. Keep your share of secrets. It's only fair since he or she has closets filled with secrets you'll probably never hear.

> **A useful tip**
>
> *High-level control men and women value their images. Therefore, it pays to bolster their egos. Make them feel good. Let them know you care and appreciate them.*

These highly controlled people value their independence, so try to give them as much freedom as you can. And, for your own sake, try not to give them any reasons to question your willingness to go along with them. They often have jealous, possessive natures that can make it very hard for them to completely trust anyone. What's more, if they feel you are drifting away from them, they'll feel they need to try to control you even more.

Establishing and maintaining a relationship with a High-level Controller can be difficult. If you find yourself smitten with one, however, remember that his or her high level of discipline is admirable and important in his or her life. Concentrate on other positive aspects of the individual's personality instead.

Loose, fleshy skin above the eyes:
No secrets—little control

Low-level—"Relaxed" skin above the eyelid

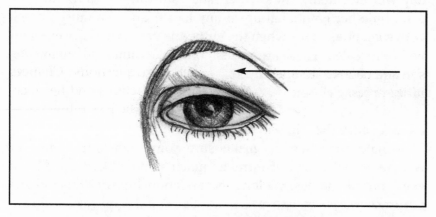

*Low control people have looser, fleshier skin
above the outside corners of their eyelids.
They're not big on facades or secrets.*

As was said in the sixties, "Let it all hang out." That's the low-control person's mantra. As you'd expect, low-control types are just the opposite of their high-control counterparts. They feel no need to control anything or anyone. They have no desire to be controlled. In fact, they want to be free spirits, unencumbered by those who want to manipulate them.

You can get to know a low-control person quickly just by talking to her. You'll discover she usually is eager to divulge lots of information about herself. Wait until you've known her longer! She truly wants everything out in the open. Nothing hidden, nothing secret and nothing mysterious. If you have a higher need for control than she does, you'll be expected to share yourself perhaps a little more than you're comfortable with.

Forget the outward poise and confident behavior we saw in High-level Controller. Low-level Controller doesn't have it. In fact,

> ## Low Control: What you see is what you get
>
> *When you meet someone with a low need for control, you know you've found someone who truly wants everything out in the open. No games. No secrets. No mysteries.*

she may act one way one minute, another the next. When she opens her mouth, everything she's ever thought about a subject might come spilling out. You may discover that she loves to think out loud, asking and answering her own questions. Chances are, her actions and her reactions will be less refined, less controlled and probably much more spontaneous than those of highly controlled people.

What's she thinking? Feeling? Worried about? You won't have to ask. With her lack of self-control, it'll soon be spread out on the table for you and the rest of the world to see.

As for honesty, while this eyelid shape does not necessarily indicate a need to be honest or need for truthfulness, a person with low control wants and expects *you* to be honest and forthcoming. In fact, she feels most comfortable with you when she believes you're making an effort to keep your emotions and feelings out in the open.

Do our control levels indicate we are a good match?

If you're open and easygoing and also don't feel the need to be in control, you'll feel right at home with a low-control man or woman, at least in this one personality facet.

On the other hand, if your need for control is higher than your partner's, you'll find yourself interacting in the exact ways—manipulating, taking advantage, directing, dominating, managing, supervising, influencing—Low-level Controller doesn't like or respect.

If having a healthy relationship with Low-level Controller is important to you, it may mean you could really benefit emotionally from being with such a person. However, you're going to have to be willing to learn new ways to communicate more openly, act a little more spontaneously and allow her the freedom she cherishes. Are those things you are willing to do?

Engaging the Low-level Controller

You'll find that men and women with low-level control needs are very easy to get to know. They keep few, if any, secrets. They're all out in the open. They will feel especially comfortable with you if you also open up and show them who you really are inside. That's what they want to see. If you honestly feel this way, tell Low-level Controller how you just hate people who want to control you. Tell them how much you also value free expression. They'll recognize a true soul mate in you.

> **Control level can be tough to see at first!**
>
> *This is one of the most important facets you can read and, unfortunately, often one of the most difficult for new face-reading students to identify. Practice watching for the telltale tight, thin skin or the loose fleshy skin above the outer eyelid.*

Holding onto the Low-level Controller

To keep your relationship with Low-level Controller strong, set aside any pretense you might have needed for a relationship with High-level Controller. Remember that a key cornerstone for a solid relationship with people who have low-level needs for control is openness. So, open up and reveal your secrets. Talk about your successes. Reveal your failures. Share your loves. Confess your fears. Lay your vulnerabilities out before the Low-level Controller and you will be valued and loved for it.

CENTRAL FACE

How to tell if your potential partner has lofty ambitions:

The inner cheek tells you how high people set their goals.

Idealistic and driven: A true competitor

High-level—Facial creases are closer together

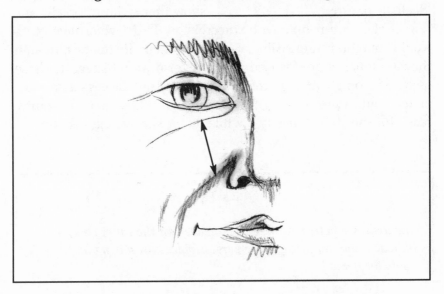

When the near-vertical distance from one crease to the next is short or the skin between is very fleshy, the person is very idealistic and very driven.

Some facial features give you important but narrowly focused information about your partner or the new man or woman on your horizon. Yet unlike other traits, this single feature—the distance from one facial crease on the cheek to another—tells you volumes.

When you find someone who has only a modest distance from one crease that traverses the cheek to the next, you've found an idealist, a true visionary and an individual who sets lofty goals. This high-level facet belongs to a person who may spend hour upon hour coming up with ways to get ahead, as well as ways to help his friends—and the world—prosper.

Next time you see a picture of Jesse Jackson, former President Jimmy Carter, Bill Cosby or Kevin Spacey, take a careful look their cheeks. All of them share this facial feature and a highly idealistic nature.

Here are people who sincerely try to do what most of us would contend is impossible. People call them dreamers, although they are much more focused than the term would suggest. These men and women strive to reach higher levels of success than most of us would dare to imagine. Despite all odds, they constantly reach for the stars. Once in a while, he or she even grabs one.

Quick Tips

The distance between these two creases on the inner cheeks indicates the importance the person places on setting high goals for herself.

Highest Levels: The closer together these creases are (and, often, the more "fleshy" this area), the higher the person's goals.

Lowest Levels: The farther apart the creases are, the more the individual needs to pursue other people's goals or wants to live without special goals.

How to measure: We measure the distances close to the nose, from one crease to the other.

Since the person with high levels of this trait is quick to formulate ideas, when things are going well he comes across as self-driven, a goal setter, a fast decision maker, a promoter, an achiever and an idea person who can be incredibly positive, hopeful and creative.

On his worst days, he can seem proud and even arrogant, plus he may feel acutely frustrated and be extremely picky. As you'll discover, being a visionary has its price.

These dreamy idealists are frequently highly competitive whether in school, in sports or enjoying their favorite pastime. They usually have winning mindsets. But it's more than that. They not only hate losing, they aren't happy unless they win big, enjoying lopsided victories.

Don't be surprised if you find this man or woman moody. These highly idealistic sorts are so full of ideas, they're never completely satisfied. No matter how much they accomplish, it's just not enough. They always have more mountains to climb, more ideas to develop, more foes to vanquish.

They're also frequently impatient. Their minds tend to be so full of ideas, so overflowing with schemes, that they feel under a lot of pressure to get it all done. They want everything done yesterday.

Unfortunately, their high levels of impatience can overflow into their relationships with other people, including yours. Don't be surprised if this High-level Idealist can become so impatient with his own life that he doesn't have time for you—or anyone else. He may become so extremely competitive, focused and self-centered as he focuses on his big dreams that your relationship with him could easily suffer, at least for a while. Don't take it personally, though. It's not you. It's him. This truly is the way he is, always was and probably always will be.

The ultimate competitors

Even though they are dreamers, these people are usually highly competitive. They tend to have a winning mindset. Not only that, they want and need to win big.

Do our idealism levels indicate we are a good match?
High-level Idealists, the world's great visionaries, have a hard time understanding people who don't hold the same grand visions. Despite the anguish it sometimes causes them, they can't imagine NOT aiming for the stars, not being obsessively competitive, not becoming overwhelmed with ideas of how they could make things better. They may have little tolerance for partners who do not share their high goals.

Do your idealism levels match? Are you as competitive and visionary as High-level Idealists? They naturally gravitate to others like themselves, people who share their dreams and goals. If that is you, go for it! If it isn't, duck and run for cover.

Engaging the High-level Idealist
You'll find you can engage the High-level Idealist rather easily. Simply dare her. If you think you're up for a heated contest, pick one of her favorite games, sports or pastimes that you have in common. Suggest that maybe you might outdo her and that she's not going to be as successful as she thinks she is. Now stand back!

You'll see her triple her usual turbocharged efforts just to prove herself and surpass you! But, an important word of caution: If you're going to make a practice of daring or questioning your new friend, make it clear that you don't doubt or question her dreams or what she stands for. She is probably looking to you for your support.

Holding onto the High-level Idealist
As long as you are prepared to share her visions and support her in attaining them—without hesitation, without question—your relationship has a good chance of flourishing.

If you start questioning what she wants by suggesting she's aiming too high or hinting that she's too starry-eyed to see reality, you'll set yourself up to fall out of her favor. Sharing her goal-setting nature would benefit your relationship the most. If you can understand her relentless inner drive toward her idealistic goals, you'll be able to share those dreams, support her causes, and encourage her so she won't give up which could be key to making a relationship with the High-level Idealist work.

In search of goals and dreams

Low-level—Greater distance between facial creases

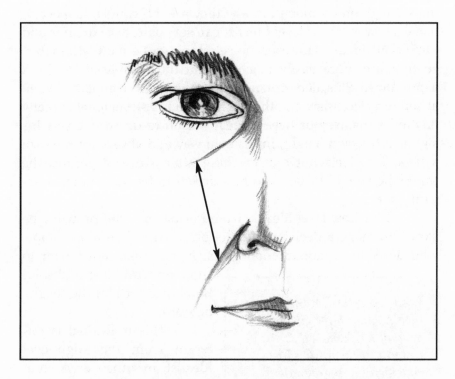

*The longer the distance between creases the less
your subject is idealistic or competitive.*

Some people don't want or need to set goals for them-selves. They don't have big dreams. They're happy pretty much the way things are. That's the Low-level Idealist.

Here's an individual who may go through his entire life not knowing what he wants to do. He possesses no special driving need to surpass others. Generally, he doesn't feel the need to com-pete and he shies away from pitting himself against others. To be fair though, it's a little more complicated than that.

Even though he may inwardly resent the way the High-level Idealist advances himself and his ideas, the Low-level Idealist finds that he gets in line behind his goal-setting counterpart and is often led by him. Since the individual generally doesn't have his own goals, he ends up working toward others' dreams.

He also tends to be a bit complacent, since he usually likes things pretty much the way they are. Of course, like everyone else, even a Low-level Idealist can set goals, have dreams and pursue his ideals. However, he sets them to be more attainable, so they are more easily reached than the High-level Idealist's aspirations. Plus, he pursues them only occasionally, when absolutely necessary. In other words, the Low-level Idealist really has to be inspired or have a great reason to do so. He sets his sights at his own height, in his own way and always for his own satisfaction. He's not one to chase after a dream because he thinks he should or because he's driven to by some outer motivating force.

Your Low-level Idealist friend or partner will probably be slower to make a decision and act on it. Also, like most people who don't have monumental goals, it may take him longer to come up with ideas and solutions that get him the results he wants.

> *Even when the Low-level Idealist does have goals, he is usually far from convinced he can attain them. He's also considerably more patient than his super-striving counterpart.*

This individual is different from the High-level Idealist in other ways, too. Even when he does have goals, he is usually not convinced he can attain them. On the plus side, you'll probably discover that he's considerably more patient than his super-striving counterpart.

Do our idealism levels indicate we are a good match?

Do you have a similarly modest need to dream and do you usually hate to compete? In this area then, you and your Low-level Idealist are a good match. On the other hand, if you're more of a dreamer or even a slightly higher level idealist, you'll probably wish this person would aim higher and show more ambition. The Low-level Idealist's seeming complacency and general contentment with the status quo could grow to become an aggravation over the long term.

Engaging the Low-level Idealist
Since this is a low-need personality facet, the best way to engage this person is not by dwelling on this particular trait, but by identifying and exploring higher needs and drives in his or her personality. Generally speaking, your relationship will be a lot more satisfying if you have many other personality traits in common with your partner.

Holding onto Low-level Idealists
If you're more of an idealist and have more clearly defined goals than your partner, don't despair if she seems overly complacent with her life. Given enough time, she'll find things that get her juices flowing and inspire her to action. In the meantime, she may be just as happy to work toward others' goals. Consequently, if you happen to have a project or goal you're working on and you want some help, you might be surprised at how much the Low-level Idealist is willing to help you attain success.

Reminder: A smile changes everything

Have you ever noticed how a smile changes a person's appearance? As a face reader, you'll have to be especially careful any time your subject is smiling or tense or showing emotions. Smiles and other expressions change the shape of the eyes, the mouth, cheeks, chin and even the nose. Your readings will be far more accurate when the subject is completely at ease and the face is composed.

UPPER EYELID

Putting others first—How to tell whether that special person in your life cares about others:

The upper eyelid reveals how compassionate he or she is.

Caring and compassionate

High-level—A curving upper eyelid

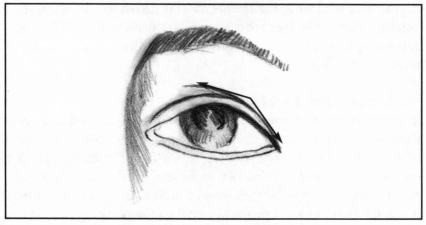

When the eyelid over the outer corner of the eyes is very rounded, you know you've found a highly compassionate partner.

If you were friendly with Cher, Jesse Jackson, Oprah Winfrey and Heather Graham, you'd realize that they all have a common trait. You couldn't help but notice how much they concern themselves with the welfare of others.

We all enjoy being the object of other people's concern and caring. Wouldn't it be wonderful to be able to spot people who naturally care so much about others' well-being that they are willing to go to great lengths for us? Psycho-Graphicology offers a telltale facial feature that indicates just that. It shows you how to identify highly compassionate people.

Men and women with sharply curving upper eyelids instinctively care for others. These highly compassionate people want to correct the world's suffering. They hate to see homelessness, poverty, war, disease or starvation. They want to rectify injustice wherever they see it. They want to make everything right. They can't deny this need in themselves, because when others hurt, they also hurt.

Quick Tips

The curves of the upper eyelids show how much a person cares about the well-being of others.

Highest Levels: The more rounded the outer eyelids, the more compassionate he is.

Lowest Levels: The flatter the eyelids, the less he worries about others and the more he cares about himself.

How to measure: Look at the curves of the upper eyelids as they move from the center of the eyes toward the outer edges of the face. The greater the curves, the higher the level of compassion.

High-level Compassionates identify and empathize with the entire world around them. Everything gets their concern and attention...people, animals, plants, even machines. What does that mean to you as you contemplate a romance or a marriage with a High-level Compassionate? It means they sincerely care about how you're doing. They want to know you're okay. They worry about you if things aren't going well for you.

Unless this individual has very rounded lower eyelids as well, she will even tend to put your needs above hers. You'll probably find that she asks what you want while subordinating her own wishes. Most of the time, with the High-level Compassionates everyone else comes first.

As you would expect, their concern for others makes it difficult for these ultra-compassionate individuals to see people or animals suffering. That's why he typically doesn't watch boxing or other rough sports, nor engage in activities that hurt others like hunting. It's just too difficult, because he naturally identifies with the pain the participants are suffering. Plus, deep inside, he's almost always cheering for the underdog.

If you spend any time at all with your rounded eyelid friends, you'll discover that compassionate people can be very demonstrative with their caring. Depending on their other traits, they may be strongly philanthropic and give freely to charities and worthy causes or they might help others with their personal and financial responsibilities. Such individuals also may be highly affectionate (especially if they have large, full lips) or be very demonstrative and physical (watch for a deep chin). Always, however, the focus for High-level Compassionates is on others.

Do our compassion levels indicate we are a good match?

To be suited for a long-term relationship with a High-level Compassionate, you would do well to share a similar level of concern for others' well-being. If you do, you'll truly appreciate and complement your partner's caring nature as few lower level compassionates can.

What if you're not as compassionate as your potential partner? You will certainly enjoy her constant interest in your well-being, but you may wonder why she seems to take such pleasure in worrying about others, instead of taking better care of herself. Be careful not to take advantage of your compassionate partner's kindness.

Engaging the High-level Compassionate

How can you use your new acquaintance's strong need to care for others to build his interest in you?

If you're sincere, show him that you can be equally caring. Demonstrate your concern for one of your favorite charities. You may want to devote some volunteer hours or make some other significant contribution to his favorite cause. Few gestures will make more of an impression on the High-level Compassionate.

At the same time, give him an opportunity to show his compassion toward you. Perhaps you could share with him a few areas in your life where you're feeling frustrated and see how he responds. As you engage his compassionate nature, you may well

Most of the time, everyone else comes first with the High-level Compassionate. Unless she has very rounded lower eyelids, you may find that she cares so much about what you want that she subordinates her own wishes.

be the recipient of some lavish attention and concern. This could turn into a happily symbiotic relationship. Highly compassionate people sincerely want to help and most of us, regardless of our own compassion level, love to be treated tenderly.

How to discover "hidden" compassion in your new interest

Sometimes you may choose a companion who appears to have small eyes with eyelids that are not particularly rounded on top. Before you jump to the conclusion that he or she is uncaring, look a little closer at the outer corners of the eyes. If you notice that the curve of the eyelids continues rounding downward beyond the corners of the eyes (see below), this person actually possesses a great deal of compassion. Why would it appear different on them? Because they have small eyes, which may hide their compassionate side.

<u>Small eyes can disguise a compassionate side</u>

"Hidden" Compassion

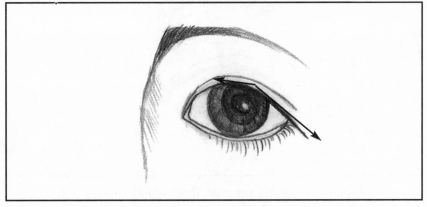

When the eyelids continue beyond the ends of the eyes and curve downward, that means the person has lots of compassion...and small eyes.

Holding onto High-level Compassionates

You'll always be able to connect with sympathetic, compassionate people by talking about your troubles. The caring part of them will enjoy listening and they will be motivated to assist you in any way they can. But I caution you: This is no way to build relationships. If that's how you constantly interact with High-level Compassionates, they'll eventually get tired of your neediness and begin to resent having such one-sided relationships with you.

If you're not a particularly compassionate soul yourself, you'll have to remember that these people have many other sides to their personalities that don't involve solving others' problems. They have their own lists of needs and things they want just like everyone else. If you want to make your relationships with High-level Compassionates work, remember their needs and desires and help them get what they want out of life. That's a surefire recipe for building a successful relationship with most people, especially with these highly compassionate individuals.

Rounded eyes on top and bottom: Signs of an adventurous spirit

High-level—"Round eyes"

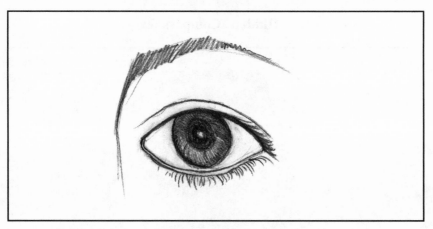

Round eyes, indicating a combination of concern for others and concern for self, are the sign of someone who is fair-minded and who also loves adventure.

When you are attracted to someone with well-rounded eyelids, top and bottom, recognize that you have come upon an individual who has a very interesting and appealing side to his or her personality. This person loves excitement and is also a born adventurer. Ask them! The person will probably smile, ask you how you know about those traits and then proudly tell you about his or her many adventures.

Not only that, these individuals tend to be eminently fairminded. They seem to have the ability to skillfully balance what they want with your needs, thereby ensuring that both of you get what you desire from the relationship.

Flat upper eyelids mean little compassion

Low-level—The eyelids have little or no curve

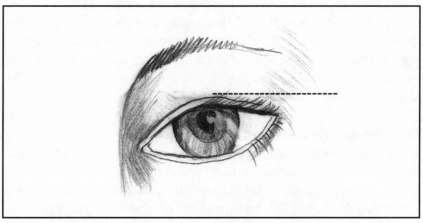

Your subjects lack concern for others when their upper eyelids, as they approach the sides of the face, are more horizontal and "flat" than curved.

Compassion? Concern for others? Those with horizontal or "flat" eyelids do not naturally have these qualities.

When the upper eyelids appear flat instead of curved, you know you've stumbled onto someone who has little or no ability to

> *Eyes which are not rounded on the top outer corner denote someone who has little or no concern for others and their problems. Depending on your needs, this person may or may not be an appropriate partner for you.*

feel others' suffering. These individuals have little empathy for others and their problems. Low-level Compassionates are not likely to help needy people they encounter on the street. Concern for the weak or the downtrodden is absent in their personalities. Their mantras are likely to be *"The homeless should take better care of themselves"* or *"They'll be fine...They know how to survive."*

Instead of falling all over himself to assist you as the High-level Compassionate would do, you'll find this person is mostly concerned about himself. You may see him as uncharitable, uncaring, even selfish. You may find he has a tendency to take advantage of others as he works to further his own interests.

A final suggestion: When your new interest has a flat upper eyelid, immediately compare it to the shape of the lower eyelid. That's the best way to get a complete picture of how this individual views other people. (We'll discuss the meaning of the shape of the lower eyelid in the next section.)

Do our eyes indicate we are a good match?

If you have rounded upper eyelids and you are by nature sympathetic, caring and compassionate, you'll find the person with flat upper eyelids is your antithesis in this area and probably not a great match. Levels of compassion, or the lack thereof, may become an issue in your relationship or they may not. Take it slowly and see how many other facets you have in common before deciding about investing in your future with this person.

If you also have flat upper eyelids and you're not a particularly caring, compassionate person without a lot of sympathy for others, the good news is that you'll understand and relate well to a person who has a similar low level of compassion. However, as you'll learn in the next section, there's also some bad news: You both probably enjoy being the center of someone else's universe.

What's your compassion level? If it's low, look for someone who has a "flat" lower eyelid and doesn't need lots of extra caring from you. If he or she also has rounded upper eyelids (high compassion), you'll be made to feel like the center of his or her universe.

And, with both of you lacking compassion, neither of you is likely to get the attention, the sympathy or the caring that you want and need. Over time, you'll both grow weary of each other's need for attention. I'd put my money on this kind of pairing not working out unless each of you puts forth extra effort to provide the emotional support the other needs.

Here's a worthwhile suggestion: If your compassion level is low, keep your eyes open for someone who has *low self-preservation,* indicated by a flat lower eyelid. That person won't want or need your constant attention. If he or she also has reasonably high compassion, this individual can make you feel like the center of the universe. You end up with the best of both worlds—you will get the attention you're looking for and he or she won't need the attention from you that you are unable to give.

Engaging the Low-level Compassionate

Low-level Compassionate is working to better her own world, not others'. The best way to get her attention involves doing something nice for her. Make her life easier. Bring her a gift. Build up her ego. Show her that you really care about her.

At the same time, you'll want to avoid sharing your troubles with her. She believes those are issues you should be handling on your own and she may not feel the inclination to help you solve them.

Holding onto the Low-level Compassionate

It's simple. Holding onto a Low-level Compassionate is really a matter of putting yourself second, not first. We all make adjustments and accommodations in our relationships; however, it may take major changes in attitude to make a success of a pairing with a Low-level Compassionate. Do you think you can you do that for a long, long time?

LOWER EYELID

How to spot a self-absorbed, "me first" person at a glance:

A well-rounded bottom eyelid means
the individual is very self-centered.

Rounded lower eyelid: Watching out for number one

High-Level—Rounded lower eyelids

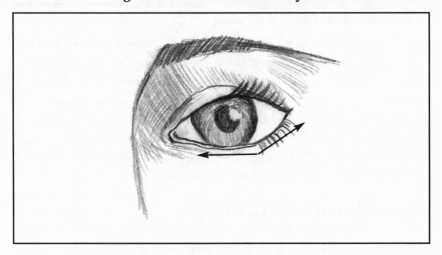

When their lower eyelids are this rounded,
they care a great deal about themselves and their welfare.

It may sound harsh, but people with very rounded lower eyelids are prone to put themselves first. Everyone else ends up farther down the list. It's especially true if they have low levels of compassion.

What makes these individuals so self-focused? People who have this feature—like Gillian Anderson, Heather Locklear and Christina Aguilera—have a strong need to protect themselves and their well-being. They regularly and instinctively stand up and fight for their own individual ideas and beliefs. Often that means there's little room for anyone else's thoughts and needs in their worlds.

Quick Tips

The roundness of the bottom eyelids (when measured from the centers of the eyes outward) indicates how self-absorbed the person is likely to be, as well as how likely he or she is to take risks.

Highest Levels: Extremely rounded lower eyelids belong to people who are very self-absorbed and hate taking risks.

Lowest Levels: "Flat" lower eyelids belong to people who like to take risks and generally put others' needs and desires first.

How to measure: Look at the curve of the lower eyelid as it moves from the center of the eye toward the outer edge of the face. The greater the rise, the more the orientation toward self-interest.

Actually, this "self-preservation" feature will tell you a lot more than that. A person with very rounded lower eyelids is a survivor. She seems to have the ability—and the strength—to make it through adversity and difficult times.

What happens when she becomes intimidated by someone or something? Usually, she responds with a natural inclination to stand up to anything that threatens her physical or mental health. You'll find this individual is very protective of her ideas, her point of view, her time, her emotions, plus her physical well-being. You probably won't find her running out into the street from between parked cars to rescue a fleeing pet (unless she absolutely knows it's safe). You also won't find a high self-preservation individual expressing her opinions if she suspects she might be exposed to any kind of abuse or criticism.

Like the Low-level Compassionate, the High-level Self-preservationist often appears to be self-centered. She considers others only after she has first taken care of herself. Don't, however, expect her to recognize that trait. She's very adept at viewing herself in the best possible light and, as a rule, she simply doesn't question her own attitudes and behaviors.

> *People with very rounded lower eyelids are survivors. They can seemingly make it through anything, often by avoiding it or putting their needs and interests before others.*

You'll find that High-level Self-preservationist wants your respect. He may not earn it, but he wants it nonetheless. That's because this individual sees everything from one point of view—his own. His welfare, his needs, his ideas, his desires, his everything comes first. Everyone else's comes, well...you know. See what happens when you change your plans without consulting him. Try challenging his ideas. Observe the fallout that follows if he ever thinks you're out to embarrass or hurt him.

He also doesn't handle criticism well. Lob a terse comment in his direction and watch what happens. You'll either see his spirit crumble before your eyes or you'll see him turn defensive and combative. When criticized, he can't help feeling acutely threatened. Stand back. At the very least, you'll find him defensive and sullen. At worst, he'll be inclined to lash out and fight back.

Engaging the High-level Self-preservationist
One great way to get a High-level Self-preservationist interested in you is to show him a great deal of respect. If you are sincere, praise his ideas or his accomplishments; tell him that you agree with his thoughts, beliefs, suggestions, interests, likes and dislikes or feelings. If you can, go the next step and actively support his plans

> *The High-level Self-preservationist sees everything from one point of view—his own. One effective way to get a Self-preservationist to notice you is to show him a lot of respect.*

and desires. Help him carry out his ideas. For example, suppose he asks you out, but his plans sound boring to you. If this guy had a lower level of self-preservation, it wouldn't be the end of the world if you offered other suggestions for the date or just turned him down. But Mr. Self-preservation, as the center of his own universe, wants and expects you to like his ideas and go along with them uncritically.

Suppose, however, you don't like his ideas. If your desire for a relationship with him is paramount, allow him his singular point of view—at first. Slowly, over time, help him recognize that there are other points of view besides his and that you have ideas and opinions of your own. If you're willing to risk it, throw out a few thoughts and suggestions of your own and see how he reacts. If he doesn't respond well, you've learned something important about him and may want to reconsider him as a potential partner. Best strategy: Instead of letting on that you don't think his ideas will work, offer some suggestions that parallel his and discuss them together. It's a lot less threatening for him and it may show him there are other good ideas out there.

Holding onto a High-level Self-preservationist

This person demands a lot of respect and deference. He wants to be the center of your universe. Said another way, he'll be much happier if your concern for him far outweighs your concern for yourself. Consequently, your time together will be much more satisfying and agreeable if your need for attention is less than his. You'll be a good match in this area if you are a compassionate, "others-focused" individual, since he is not. Finally, his need to protect himself means he hates criticism, so he'll like you a lot more if you are not a judgmental, critical sort.

Hints Spotting High-level Compassionates

The most compassionate people have eyes with very rounded upper eyelids. Anytime you see either eyes that are rounded top and bottom *or* are round on top and more "flat" on the bottom, you have uncovered a very caring soul.

Hints for Spotting Low-level Compassionates

Eyes belonging to the least compassionate people may be flat or rounded on the bottom, but always appear flat on top. You'll know that you've located a Low-level Compassionate when you see someone with eyes that:

> - appear to rise the closer they get to the side of the face, like a cat's or,
> - appear very narrow, as if in a natural squint even when at rest, since both the top and bottom eyelids are "flat."

Straight lower eyelid: Little concern for self

Low-level Self-preservation—The "flat" lower eyelid

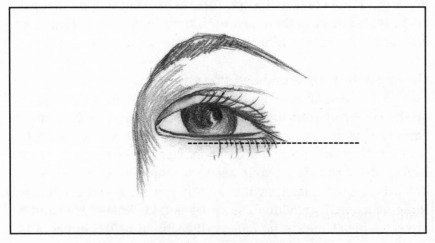

The lower eyelids on the outer edges of the eyes
appear flat or curve only very slightly upward on
people who care little about their own well-being.

When the bottoms of an individual's eyes appear "flat," (that is, the lower eyelid is quite straight from its center as it approaches the side of the face), you can expect that the person you're studying puts others ahead of herself. She sincerely believes that others' needs and wants are more significant than her own.

If you watch her interactions with colleagues at work or with friends, you may wonder why she doesn't wear a T-shirt that says *"Walk all over me"* on the front. It is possible that she is easily taken advantage of. She simply doesn't place a high value on her well-being, whether it's her physical, emotional or mental health. Generally, you'll find that she thinks her needs are a low priority.

> *Not one to concern herself with her own physical or emotional well-being, a Low-level Self-preservationist may also occasionally put herself in risky—even dangerous—situations.*

For example, it's probably a huge challenge for her to stand up for herself, even though inaction can tear her apart inside. She seems incapable of helping herself even when she clearly needs to take action. As a result, she easily can be taken advantage of by colleagues, friends and lovers.

> **Read eyes very carefully.**
>
> *Eyes, like some other parts of the face, change almost moment to moment. A smile or exposure to bright lights can cause squinting, transforming a round eye into one that appears flat on the top and bottom. For most accurate results, read subjects' eyes only when they're at rest and their faces are expressionless.*

Since a Low-level Self-preservationist doesn't concern herself with (or much care about) her physical safety and well-being, she might also put herself in risky, even dangerous situations. She's the kind of person who jumps into things that would give others with higher levels of self-preservation serious pause. She doesn't feel fear the way most of us do and she usually doesn't consider whether she could injure herself. You might think of her as a hero type. Many times, those individuals who spontaneously rush into burning buildings or dive into icy water to rescue people possess low levels of self-preservation.

Do our self-preservation levels indicate we are a good match?

Just as high self-preservation types do well with high compassion people who show concern for them and give them the attention they want, low self-preservation people will frequently feel more comfortable with low compassion individuals. That's because they just don't want people worrying about and fussing over them.

Engaging the Low-level Self-preservationist

This is not the kind of trait you can "play" to. You'd be better off finding other facial features and personality traits indicating needs she has that you can help fill.

Holding onto the Low-level Self-preservationist

Once you've become involved with someone who displays the traits of low self-preservation, you'll see what an easy target she can be for people who want to take advantage of her. If you care for this person, you could find yourself wanting to help her stand up for herself and set realistic, protective boundaries. In fact, you could help her a lot in this area since it's not in her nature to do so. Eventually, with your help and encouragement, she may start to take better care of herself.

Complementary eye shapes may indicate you are choosing the right partner

As I have explained, one way you can choose the right person for you is by examining his or her eye shapes. An overview of eye types that complement each other follow on the next two pages.

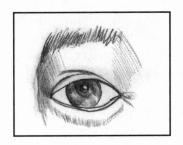

Partner A

People with very curved upper and lower eyelids (compassionate with high level of self-preservation) are especially suited...

Partner B

for others with similarly rounded eyelids (and similar personality traits)

A person with round eyes (indicating high compassion and high self-preservation) is well matched in these two areas with another person who has similar eyes as shown in the drawing above. In this case, both people have a comparable need to balance their concern for other people as well as for themselves. Note: While Partner A's eyes don't have to have the same exact shape as Partner B, the top *and* bottom eyelids of both people should be equally curved, indicating each person has a balanced regard for others and self.

Partner A

Rounded upper lids (compassionate) combined with 'flat' lower eyelids (low self-preservation) are compatible with...

Partner B

rounded lower eyelids (a need for others' caring) and 'flatter' upper eyelids (suggests a less caring nature) but not as well matched...

Partner C

for partner C who has both rounded lower and upper eyelids (since Partner A doesn't need others' caring concern).

As depicted in the drawing on the bottom of the previous page, when low self-preservation people are also very compassionate (Partner A), the best match is someone who has a high level of self-preservation. Individuals who have high compassion (Partner C) are not as well suited, however, since Low-level Self-preservationists do not need or appreciate caring partners' constant concern.

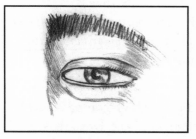

Partner A

When both top and bottom lids are relatively flat (little concern for self or others)...

Partner B

others with similar eyelid shapes (and traits) are often the most suitable mates.

When both compassion and self-preservation are low, like Partner A in the drawings above, this person is not especially concerned about himself or others. A good match for this individual is generally someone of the same or similar low compassion and self-preservation levels—someone who neither needs others' concern nor wants to give it.

NOSE TIP

How to discover a partner who criticizes and one who doesn't:

When the nose tip is pointed, so are his or her comments.

The sharp nose: The sharp critic

High-Level—Narrow-tip nose

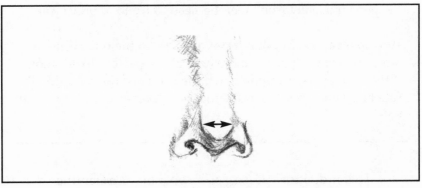

*Whether the nostrils of the nose are wide or
narrow, a narrow nose tip is your clue that
this person wants to improve you.*

You've probably noticed that some people have noses with very narrow tips. You may have observed that Jodie Foster, Maria Shriver, Jim Carrey and Rick Schroder all have relatively pointed noses. What does it mean?

A narrow nose tip is a sign that you're looking at a person who instinctively wants to help others improve their lives. Very often, this need to improve others is expressed in what may feel to friends and lovers like criticism.

Quick Tips

The width of the nose tip is your gauge of how critical this person will be.

Highest Levels: When the nose tip is very narrow (it may appear almost pointed), the person is naturally very critical.

Lowest Levels: When the nose tip is wide from side to side, the person usually won't feel the need to try to improve you.

How to measure: Measure from one side to the other. The more narrow the tip, the more critical the person. In addition, if there's a crease running down the center of the nose tip, it's safe to assume that the individual has developed a very critical nature.

This individual possesses a constant, unrelenting drive (if you ask him, he may call it a responsibility) to point out faults while hoping that the people on the other end of his criticism will use his guidance to improve themselves.

To most of us, such comments frequently sound judgmental and critical. If you're around a partner like this for any length of time, you may start to feel you're under attack or that you're just not measuring up to their standards.

After your initial wincing reaction to his criticism, if you're willing to look objectively at what's being said, you will very often discover that your sharp-nosed friend is accurate. You may even develop a grudging respect for his ability to know what's not right about what you've said or done and how it can be corrected.

This trait is a heavy burden to possess. Though the High-level Critic seems to focus on others' flaws, he is also seldom completely satisfied with any aspect of his own life. Often faults, weaknesses and shortcomings are just about all he sees, not to mention mistakes, inaccuracies, inconsistencies, problems and imperfections—in both others and himself. He just naturally knows which things could be better and often he knows how to go about improving them. It may be hard to see, but the High-level Critic doesn't want to upset or offend people. What he really wants is to make an important, worthwhile contribution to their lives.

Believe it or not, depending on their other personality traits, critical people don't always share their thoughts. For example, if your critical boyfriend or girlfriend has high self-control, he'll keep his thoughts to himself unless he's absolutely overcome with the need to express himself.

As you get to know him better, you may also find that he is hard to please—and quick to judge. He always strives for excellence, wants things at their very best and consequently he zeros in on problems right away. A quick, accurate evaluator, especially in areas where he has experience and abilities, this individual is a true perfectionist. He sees everything as it could be and he does what he can to make it just that way. If it makes you feel any better, he's as hard on himself as he is on you.

"All she does is criticize!"

Those critical remarks can sting, especially when they come from someone you care about. So there's only one way to look at them: Remember that highly critical people always criticize to be of benefit...they want to help you, not point out your errors and short-comings just to hurt your feelings. They have a talent for seeing imperfections. Do your best to accept their criticisms, even if they smart a little, since there's probably some truth there.

Do our nose tips indicate we are a good match?
In the case of this particular trait, it's really not a matter of whether your nose tips match. It's more a question of how well you are able to handle criticism from the special person in your life. If you really, honestly don't mind it, great, you two could be a good match in this area. On the other hand, if you're sensitive to blunt comments, honest judgments and out-and-out criticism, you might want to reconsider this relationship. Remember, with the High-level Critic it'll be an ongoing, regular aspect of your partnership. The question is: Do you need this in your life? Or, if you're really, truly crazy about him, can you learn to accept his criticism with equanimity?

Here's my suggestion: Figure out how critical of yourself you are. If you are a perfectionist already and find yourself falling short of your own standards, you don't need the most important person in your life also telling you how you could improve. On the other hand, if you are someone who doesn't engage in self-criticism, and you already know you handle occasional comments and criticisms easily, then you may be able to form and maintain a good relationship with this person.

Don't be fooled: He's still a critic

High-level: Narrow tip nose with wide nostrils

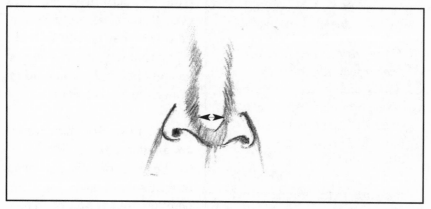

Although the nostrils here look wider, the tip is still narrow. This person is also a High-level Critic.

Engaging the High-level Critic

Highly critical people love to do one thing—critique. If you want to engage an individual with this trait and if you really want honest (sometimes brutal) feedback on something you care about, you could ask the High-level Critic for his opinion. In the early stages of a relationship, he may tend to hold back so as not to scare you away. So tell him to be honest, that you really want his opinion. He'll enjoy the opportunity to relax and show his true self and make a contribution to your life.

Holding onto the High-level Critic

Not surprisingly, highly critical people often don't feel appreciated, because many people simply can't cope with their criticisms. If you can, do something many people would never consider: Thank him for his comments. Show that you appreciate his thoughts and efforts to help you improve.

If you're afraid that opening yourself up to the High-level Critic's comments will be too emotionally upsetting, you can minimize the possibility of an onslaught. Limit his comments by asking for his opinions on specific areas. For example, if you respect his artistic sense and have a completed painting you would like him to comment on, don't just say "Have at it" and risk his telling you that you should trade in your brushes. Instead, ask him specific questions about your color palette, the subject or the lighting. This will show him that you value the contributions he can make. At the same time, it will put him on notice that, while you appreciate his candor, *you will decide what subjects are appropriate* for his critical attention.

The wide nose tip: "Live and let live"

Low-level—Not a natural critic

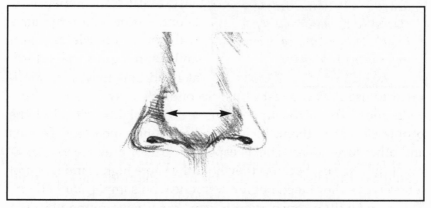

On an uncritical person, the tip of the nose will appear wide. But watch for a vertical telltale crease, indicating this individual has been taught to be highly critical.

Some people (such as David Duchovny, Pierce Brosnan, Jon Bon Jovi, Chris Rock, Jerry Rice, Tom Hanks and Kevin Bacon) have no real desire or need to constructively criticize people, things or situations. These are the people with wide nose tips (and no vertical creases that divide the nose tip in half).

Among such people you'll find neither the drive nor the interest nor the ability to criticize. You'll find the mantra of these men and women is "live and let live." Instead of feeling the need to improve others through criticism, they come across as very accepting and tolerant individuals. They naturally want to accept you just the way you are. These Low-level Critics don't see your frailties. In fact, they may want to believe you don't have any.

To be fair, you probably know people who have wide nose tips who are also fault-finding and highly critical. They just jump right in, offering their opinions of how things could be better. How can that be?

As you'll see, there are a number of good reasons why many wide-nose-tip persons act like narrow-nose-tip people, reasons you'll want to remember if you pursue relationships with them. First, even wide-nose-tip folks, with no discernible creases, feel perfectly free to criticize in areas where they have firsthand experience or talent. After all, they have real-world knowledge and understanding of the subject at hand and they're as motivated to use it as the rest of us. Second, it's easy for all people—wide-tipped or narrow-tipped noses—to be highly critical of the people closest to them, including their family members, friends and other loved ones. This is especially true if they are very critical of themselves, because they hold the same high standards, not for everyone they meet, but for everyone who's important to them. This may be little consolation to you, but if you are the object of these people's critical remarks, remember it's only because they love you.

> *You'll find individuals with wide-tipped noses can also be highly critical of others, but usually only of the people closest to them, including their family members, friends and other loved ones.*

Another reason wide-nose-tip people can seem critical may be because they learned from others to point out imperfections. This lesson—from discerning and critical parents, teachers or other influential people—may have been drilled into their heads over and over until they became just as critical. Often, these people end up with a telltale crease in their nose, but not always.

Finally, you'll find that people who are unhappy, whatever the shape of their nose tip, often tend to take their dissatisfactions out on others by being critical. Crankiness quickly turns into faultfinding and carping.

Do our nose tips indicate we are a good match?

If you're already a very self-critical sort—trying to be perfect, always working at doing things "right," getting mad at yourself when you make mistakes—a non-judgmental person will feel a lot more comfortable to you than a person who loves to find fault. He or she will make you feel accepted for who you are, shortcomings, imperfections and all. At least for a while....

As your relationship progresses, however, this accepting man or woman may start to see you differently. Over time, the longer you know each other, the less immune you are to criticism. The closer you get, the more your non-critical friend's expectations will change as you shift from being a friend or a date to a full-fledged spouse or partner. Call it human nature, but as you grow closer and become a part of each other's lives, you'll probably be subject to some level of criticism and faultfinding.

Engaging the Low-level Critic

Low-level criticism is another personality trait that is difficult to connect with. (I suppose you could walk right up to a person and say *"Gee, you look like you don't want to improve me. I'll bet criticizing me is the last thing on YOUR mind!"* then see what he or she does.) No, it would be wiser for you to find other personality facets you can connect with, ones that have a stronger influence on the individual's personality.

MOUTH CORNERS

**How to learn whether your new love interest
views a glass as half full or half empty:**

Want to be with an optimist? Look at the corners of the mouth.

<u>Upturned mouth: The Optimist</u>

High-level—A subtle, natural smile

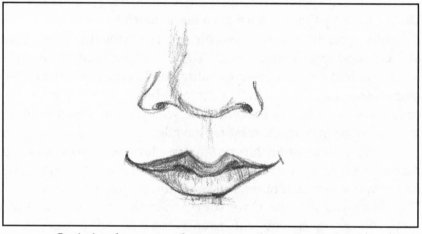

*Optimists have a gentle upturn to the corners of their
mouths that almost makes them look like they're
smiling, even when their faces are at rest.*

The traits of optimism and pessimism are easy to spot and tell you a great deal about whether you'll want to be around your potential new partner or not. The challenge here is getting the new person in your life to relax his or her mouth enough so you can get an accurate reading.

You'll find it's especially easy to spot people who think positively. Eternal optimists have mouths that turn up fairly sharply at the ends. (Take a look at Meg Ryan, Ben Affleck, Matthew McConaughey or Bill Cosby and you will see what I mean.) These individuals have very positive views of life; they fully expect that only good will prevail.

Quick Tips

The corners of the mouth tell you if the person is a cockeyed optimist, a died-in-the-wool pessimist or something in-between.

Highest Levels: The optimist has a mouth with corners that curve upward, as if in a perpetual smile.

Lowest Levels: The pessimist's mouth turns down at the ends, in a slight or obvious perpetual frown. The whole mouth may appear to turn down.

How to measure: The more the corners go up or down, the more the person anticipates positive results (optimism) or negative results (pessimism).

You'll probably enjoy these people because they bring a very positive, upbeat feeling to just about any situation. They are often physically and mentally "up" and willingly share their enthusiasm. Events and occasions are looked forward to and usually they talk in very positive terms about anything in which they're interested.

For optimists, hope, faith and positive thinking are the philosophies by which they live their lives. So much so in fact, that sometimes you may wonder if they are really observing this world's reality or some better universe. No matter how bad things may look to you, eternal optimists are always willing to shield their eyes against harsh reality and see the world through rose-colored glasses.

Even when everyone else insists nothing can be done, the optimist blithely ignores the odds, charges ahead and attempts to do what most people would consider the impossible. As a result, where others fail, he or she often succeeds.

Despite discouraging facts and even in the face of huge obstacles, in their hearts optimists believe nothing bad will happen.

> *Over the course of our lives, faced with challenges or adversity, some of us slowly become pessimistic. The good news is that, with a little self-discipline, anyone can shift from a pessimistic outlook and become a positive thinker once again.*

While they're not always correct, of course, their hopeful expectations lead to desired positive results more often than people who expect less could ever imagine.

The Optimist's biggest enemy—his only real enemy—is disappointment. Too much negativity and disappointment can eventually cool down his optimism and perhaps even turn it into pessimism. I believe we are all born optimists. Over the course of our lives, faced with too many difficult challenges or adversity, some of us slowly become pessimistic. We start expecting "bad" things to happen. The good news is that, with a little self-discipline, anyone can shift from a pessimistic outlook to become a positive thinker once again. It just takes practice to identify the positive aspects and the good side of any situation until it's what we naturally and automatically hone in on.

Do our mouth shapes indicate we are a good match?

Optimists are easily offended by pessimists. Negative thinking wears on them. Optimists also don't understand or appreciate why others would expect anything but the best outcomes. So if you're inclined to see only the negative side of life, don't expect anyone who looks through rose-colored glasses to be attracted to you. On the other hand, if you are optimistic in your outlook, you'll maintain your energy and enthusiasm by surrounding yourself with others who possess the same or a similar positive approach to life.

Engaging the Optimist

If you want to attract an optimist's attention and start earning his interest and respect, you'll need to be upbeat and confident. Just as important, you'll need to share in his enthusiasm for life. Join with him in his expectations of a sunny, promising future. Show him you're just as excited about life as he is. Already, you two sound like a great couple!

Holding onto the Optimist

If you're also a positive thinker, you've already got a lot of the glue you need to stay attached to this partner, assuming you're a good match in other ways. Stay positive, recognizing the importance of this trait you have in common. After all, how many times in your life do you find someone with as refreshing an outlook as the optimist?

If you're not a positive thinker—if you're a negative soul and you have no intentions of changing your outlook—you'd best move on early, for both your sakes. The Optimist is not the partner for you. As much as you might enjoy his upbeat attitude, if you're not changing in a positive direction, he'll grow weary of your negativity.

Downturned mouth: The Pessimist

Low-level—The built-in frown

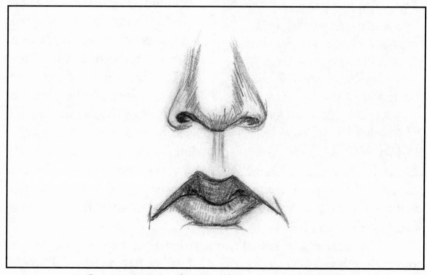

On pessimists, the mouth corners turn down
slightly or alot. (Make sure to watch for this
trait when their mouths are at rest).

In extreme cases, the Pessimist appears to be wearing a permanent frown. In most cases, the corners of her mouth turn slightly downward at the ends. As you might imagine, that's a sign that this individual not only expects the worst, but she may also be actively looking for the worst to justify her point of view.

The true Pessimist anticipates being disappointed and she experiences that feeling right from the beginning of a situation. That way, she can't be let down or hurt later on.

Spend any length of time in their presence and you'll discover that pessimists often cast a negative pall on everything and everyone. They naturally look at and talk about the sorry side of life: the bad news, the sad stories, their latest misfortunes, how tough life is. And if they can't find the bad in the situation at hand, they may recall an old incident, create something or jump on a small detail and blow up its negative attributes.

Pessimists can show enthusiasm or get excited about life, events or people, but before they do they frequently have a habit of uncovering and examining all possible negative aspects. They'll portray their potential new interests in as negative a light as they can. Finally, they begin the slow, deliberate process of mentally building up these things they've worked so hard to pull apart. Since they don't want to be disappointed, however, one thing doesn't change: Until the point when the events occur successfully or they get what they want, pessimists never completely let go of their expectations that they will fail.

> *All is not lost for the Pessimist. Remember, this individual can change... With just a little practice he can once again become the card-carrying Optimist he was born to be. The keys: the Pessimist has to want to change and see life differently.*

You can easily spot the most extreme pessimists. To see examples of how this trait looks on a face, notice pictures of World War II Nazi Joseph Goebbels or politicians Richard Nixon and George Wallace. If you want to find an example closer to home, look for a person who seems depressed, glum, cautious or very serious. Life is a burden for the pessimist. People can't be counted on. The job is not going well and never will. There's nothing to look forward to. And if things *are* going well? Unfortunately, the Pessimist almost never sees the good side. She just knows things

Pessimists tend to like more cheerful, confident and encouraging people. Perhaps that's because deep down they really want to be happy and enthusiastic about life. Unfortunately, pessimists and optimists are not always a comfortable match.

will fail. She expects and almost looks forward to disaster. Even if it doesn't happen, she spends a large part of her life fearing it. No wonder she is easily depressed!

All is not lost for the Pessimist. Remember, she can change...with just a little practice she can once again become the sunny optimist she was born to be. The key is she has to want to change and view life differently. She has to realize there's another, more satisfying way to live out her days. It just takes will power, a little time and constant practice. I know, because I've done it.

Do our mouth shapes indicate we are a good match?

I'm convinced that deep down, everyone wants to be happy and enthusiastic about life. This would explain why pessimists tend to gravitate toward more cheerful, confident and encouraging people. Unfortunately, optimists and pessimists are not usually well-suited for each other. Died-in-the-wool pessimists are frequently better paired to other confirmed pessimists, because of their common outlooks. At the same time, most optimists (except the highest level) can be comfortable with mild (not severe) pessimists. As long as their outlooks don't diverge too much, both partners will learn to co-exist and the more negatively inclined partner may even raise his expectations.

Engaging the Pessimist

When you are attracted to and want to connect with a pessimist, your best approach is to sound moderately optimistic. Be confident and content without going over the top. Even though he may wonder aloud or silently about your self-assuredness, you'll find that he will like your positive attitude and he'll naturally want to spend time with you. Don't go too far, however. If you do, you could easily send your newfound, low-energy friend running in the other direction.

UPPER LIP

How to discover who's affectionate...and who's not:

The size of the upper lip tells you how
much affection someone will lavish upon you.

The affectionate upper lip

High-Level—The upper lip is full and prominent

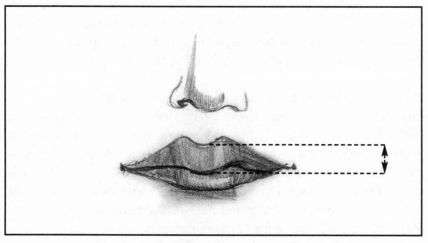

*People with large upper lips want your praise and
acceptance and they will try to get it by showering
you with attention and affection.*

Can you guess what Julia Roberts, Monica Lewinsky, Pamela Anderson Lee, Courtney Love, Jimmy Carter, Barbra Streisand and Toni Braxton all have in common? A quick look at their faces will tell you they all have full upper lips.

You'll find that men and women who have upper lips that rise high above their mouths also have strong, unrelenting needs to be accepted by others. They need to influence people, have their ideas appreciated and their advice taken.

This High-level Affectionate has found that he can get that acceptance and affect others by enthusiastically showing that he likes them. That's why you'll often find a person with a prominent upper lip paying you more attention than you might think appropriate. That's his way of putting you at ease, so you will accept him as well as accept what he has to say.

Large-upper-lipped people tend to love to talk. They will also go to extremes in hopes of getting reactions just so you'll notice them. They might share their thoughts and feelings more earnestly or more energetically than you'd expect. They may present themselves as outgoing, gushing individuals.

You may find people with large upper lips showing off or behaving uninhibitedly to get attention. If they are motivated by touch, they may engage you physically, too, with hardy handshakes, enthusiastic hugs or spirited kisses. The High-level Affectionate may stand a little closer to you than you'd like. They may attempt to engage you with flattery or use their charm on

---

Quick Tips

The height of the upper lip is your cue to how outgoing and affectionate a person is.

Highest Levels: The most affectionate, attention-lavishing people have upper lips that rise proportionately high above their mouths.

Lowest Levels: Upper lips on people who are the least affectionate and most reserved rise only slightly or their upper lips are thin or virtually non-existent.

How to measure: Study the distance from the line where the upper and lower lips meet to where the upper lip ends, near the center of the mouth.

you. You might find them speaking a little louder than seems appropriate or talking more than you'd expect. You may be surprised to receive unsolicited gifts, too. In their unrestrained efforts to seek your acceptance, you might decide their behavior is a bit obnoxious, especially if you compare it with the restraint that people with thinner lips exhibit or if you are a more reserved person.

One of the worst things you can do to people who sport full upper lips is ignore them. It hurts them deeply. Two of their main desires are to be noticed and to be accepted. When you don't pay them the attention they want and need, they have to find others who will. This is a strong personality trait that they cannot disregard.

Do our upper lips indicate we are a match?

If you like lots of attention and you need lots of approval from others (perhaps you have a large lower lip) you'll probably enjoy— or at least feel fairly comfortable with—people who sport these extravagant upper lips. After all, the kind of appreciation they bestow can feel really good. What could be better than being the center of someone's universe?

High-Level Affectionates get along best with people who love to receive their endless stream of affection. So if you're the kind of person who needs a lot of praise, acceptance and attention, you might just be a good fit with this type of individual.

Engaging the High-level Affectionate

This is one person you may not have to engage. It often happens that he or she will walk right up to you and start a conversation before you know what happened. Could there be an easier way to begin a relationship?

You may get a glimmer sometimes that this person is a little insecure. Perhaps. What you may be seeing is that inside this individual is a person who believes he deserves others' attention and respect. Naturally he is easily upset when people disregard him or don't pay him the attention he feels he deserves. Since he is in large part driven by the need to be accepted by anyone he cares for, don't be surprised if he takes rejection badly. Of course, few of us take rejection well. But for this acceptance-focused soul, it's especially painful.

Thin upper lip: The "quietly affectionate"

Low-level—Thin upper lip

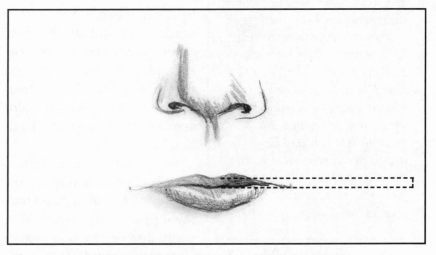

When the mouth is at rest, this person will appear to have only a very thin upper lip.

When you find someone with a small or thin upper lip as the center of attention at a gathering, it won't be because that individual is seeking attention. He or she doesn't want or need it.

Think about people you know with small or nonexistent upper lips. Aren't they invariably the people who tend to stand back on the fringes of a group? Don't they tend to say as little as possible, to stay quiet, to sit back and watch others? Aren't they often the people you'd describe as introverted?

Unlike their lush-lipped counterparts, people with proportionately thin upper lips have no need to influence people around them in order to get attention. Some might say these Low-level

Affectionates are standoffish or aloof. At their cores they are observers, watching all those people who love to get and give attention. They usually don't want to get involved. It can even be difficult for them to commit themselves to others. Why? Because they are not comfortable feeling that they owe anyone anything, including acceptance, praise or appreciation. Usually, they also don't feel the need to charm or engage people unless they have specific reasons.

> *The man or woman with thin upper lips isn't one for lots of conversation. If you want to talk, it may take some effort to start a conversation. You could find it even harder to keep it going long enough to draw him or her out. But your efforts can pay big dividends...Eventually your thin-lipped love interest will feel more comfortable around you and will open up.*

Since this is a low-level need, they are motivated much more strongly by their other personality traits. For example, without a high need for touch you won't find them offering strangers or mere acquaintances a handshake or a hug.

Want a demonstrative mate? You probably won't find one here among the narrow-lipped. These people generally don't show many overt signs of affection for others. They're just too reserved. If you want their acceptance or affection, you'll have to work for it.

Do our upper lips indicate we are a good match?
Do you enjoy people who keep to themselves, individuals who tend to be reserved and are often more observers than participants? If so, then you could be happy with this man or woman, at least in this particular area. However, if you require a great deal of affection, you may find your needs not being met.

Engaging the Low-Level Affectionate
Are you really prepared to cope with the lack of attention you'll receive from this individual? Really? You'll often find your thin-lipped, prospective partner either hanging back, staying pretty much to himself or talking comfortably to only his closest friends. (He finds it uncomfortable venturing too far out of his shell.)

Attracting this person's attention isn't usually difficult. While he may feel more secure when he stays to himself, he also enjoys interesting conversation and wants people with whom to interact, both friends and lovers. So you should be able to engage his attention quietly, with about as much enthusiasm as he is putting out. Try to match his low-octane energy level. Honor his need to be reserved and allow him to be his standoffish self by asking him a few easy-to-answer questions just to break the ice.

Don't expect lots of conversation in return. In fact, it may take some work on your part to keep the conversation going and draw him out. Your efforts can pay big dividends, however, as he grows more comfortable around you and starts to open up. The cliché states "Still waters run deep" and that may be the case with the thin-lipped individual to whom you are attracted. Perhaps you will discover real seriousness and depth in this potential partner.

One more thing. Remember how thin-lipped individuals don't enjoy feeling they owe anyone anything? The reason is that they like to keep all "accounts balanced." That way, they don't have to go out of their way to reciprocate for others. If you do something nice for her, 1) don't make it too grand or extravagant and 2) let her know she won't need to pay you back. This should go a long way toward ensuring that she enjoys your thoughtfulness and helping her comfortably accept your gift without feeling the obligation to respond in kind.

Holding onto the Low-level Affectionate

Men and women with thin upper lips often stay very much to themselves for their whole lives. Let's not hold out any false hopes. They will never be extroverts. Even if you end up married to one, he or she may never be the conversationalist you want. She usually won't go out of her way to engage you in conversation unless there's something in particular she wants to communicate or unless she feels an occasional need to open up. Be prepared to spend a lot of quiet time, even when you're together. If you are comfortable engaging in a "companionable silence," this may be the right partner for you.

LOWER LIP

How to tell how much attention your partner requires:

A large lower lip signifies a strong need to be noticed.

The full lower lip: Hungry for praise and attention

High-level—Full lower lip

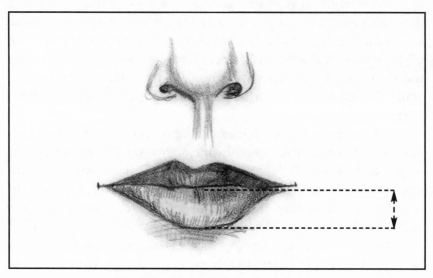

*You'll find people with large lower
lips love getting your attention.*

When you are attracted to a man or woman with a deep
lower lip, you'll almost invariably find that he or she can be very
talkative or are quite communicative in other ways.

You'll realize quickly that one of this individual's most
obvious characteristics is her need to receive attention from those
around her. The more notice, the better; the more people who
offer it, the better.

A person with this trait, however, wants more than attention. She displays an unrelenting craving for acceptance and

feedback plus a high-level need for praise, appreciation and recognition. She'll look for and happily accept them wherever and whenever she finds these kinds of positive attentions and from anyone, whether the person is important to her or not. When she is the object of such courtship and wooing, be it romantic or platonic, she feels as if she's being bathed in pure love. Suddenly, she feels completely content with herself, life seems glorious and everyone around her becomes a magnificent human being.

Can you think of anyone you know with a large lower lip? You probably didn't know it at the time, but you've also seen this strong need to receive attention on the faces of Matt Damon, Melanie Griffith, Marilyn Monroe, Diane Sawyer, Selena and Howard Stern, to name just a few.

These well-known people, like other large-lower-lipped men and women, usually like to talk. Why? Because by engaging or involving others through communications, they elicit reactions and further interaction. Those responses help satisfy their relentless need for attention and acceptance.

Quick Tips

The depth of the lower lip tells you how much attention, praise and acceptance a person needs to receive from others.

Highest Levels: When the lip appears large and full in proportion to the rest of the facial features including the upper lip, you can bet your friend's need for others' acceptance is strong.

Lowest Levels: When the lower lip is thin or non-existent, proportionately, you know this individual is not needy for your attention or acceptance.

How to measure: We assess the distance from the line where the lips meet down to the lower edge of the lip, near the center of the mouth.

An Attention Needer, she seems willing to go to any extreme to ensure that you notice her. Frequently a non-stop talker, she may also speak louder than seems necessary. If you start to look away, she may move so your gaze stays focused on her or she might take a different tack by entertaining you with amusing noises or funny faces and the like. She might even tease you or take the liberty of pulling on your sleeve, all for the same end...to get your attention.

There's nothing people with large lower lips want more than applause. Even when they do nothing, they want and need positive recognition. They crave the attention that being in the spotlight brings them, where they can be acknowledged by others and have praise and recognition heaped upon them.

> *Want your praise-motivated love interest to be totally devoted to you? Lavish him or her with sincere praise. Take notice and point out anything she's done that you appreciate.*

Want him to follow you to the ends of the earth? Be lavish with praise. Want him to act his very best? Always recognize him for anything he's done that you appreciate. You'll be rewarded with a partner who is happy, motivated and full of life.

Unfortunately, with the opposite scenario—if he doesn't get the praise he needs—he'll quickly lose his spark and wither like a dying flower. He'll become unhappy, perhaps even depressed. Attention is a key source of his enthusiasm, his liveliness. Cut it off and he suffers.

You're going to find that most people's lower lips are larger than their upper lips. In other words, the majority of people in this world want to RECEIVE more affection and praise than they want to GIVE. (Seems unfair, doesn't it?) If you care about a full lower-lipped individual, don't worry about how much attention she's giving you. Instead, concentrate on what she needs more than almost anything in her life—your attention. Lavish her with it as much as you can.

As you might expect, one of the greatest fears for anyone with a high need to receive attention is rejection. For someone who loves acceptance and favor, few things are as painful. Rejection not only means losing face, but it also can lead to a significant erosion in self-confidence. This is true for all of us mortals, but it is exacerbated in attention-loving individuals.

If you find you have to let go of this man or woman, be very mindful of the significance of every word you utter, every gesture you make as you break off the relationship. I am not exaggerating when I say that for this person, rejection can be devastating.

Engaging the Attention Needer

Like the full upper-lipped person driven to shower affection on others, you may not have to engage this man or woman at all. Once she senses that you're able and willing to give her the attention she needs, it may be only a matter of moments before *she's* engaged *you*.

However, what if this scenario hasn't happened? Let's say you're attracted to her and want to meet her but she doesn't seem, at this particular time, to be needing your attention. The best thing you can do is find ways to be even more mindful. Remember, this person is most compatible with people who GIVE lots of attention, and the larger her lower lip, the more of it she craves. Start up a conversation with her. Praise her for something, even if it seems minor. Show her you have the ability to satisfy her need for appreciation.

> *Be warned...If you want a relationship with an Attention Needer to last, one of the most important things you can do is to provide the positive feedback your mate needs. If you're really committed, you should expect to offer regular praise, acceptance, attention and affection.*

She can't help but like you for it! If you can demonstrate that you're a fountain of praise, you have a starting place to begin a new, rewarding relationship.

Holding onto the Attention Needer

One thing that has a tendency to kill a relationship is when one partner starts taking the other for granted. People with deep lower lips especially hate being taken for granted, more than just about anyone else in the universe. Be warned: Once you're committed to this man or woman, you'll be on constant call to offer praise, acceptance, attention and affection. If you're in this relationship for the long haul, one of your most important roles will be to provide the constant, positive feedback your mate needs.

Large-lower-lipped individuals frequently take negative feedback poorly and may react very strongly to anything you say that doesn't support their need for praise and attention. Be very careful how you find fault. If you have to criticize them, learn to do it gingerly and with a very light touch. Learn to phrase your comments diplomatically if you want to get results, yet avoid hurting your friend or partner.

Finally, learn to provide continual feedback. The partner you've chosen needs it. He or she even yearns for it (though this probably would never be admitted to you). This special feature, by the way, will be a telling aspect of your suitability in this area. My bet is, if you have narrow lips, you won't want to continually have to offer positive feedback to your partner. And that's why two people who both have large lips make a more compatible couple.

The thin lower lip: Wants to be out of the limelight

Low-level—Thin lower lip

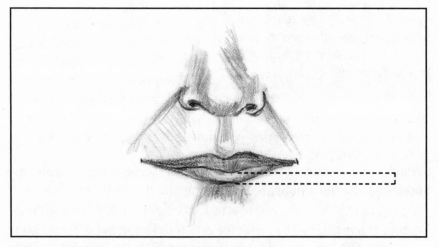

You'll find people with thin lower lips keep a very low profile...and don't want too much attention most of the time.

Just as the large-lower-lipped person loves to bathe in the glow of the spotlight, a person with a thin or hidden lower lip avoids drawing attention to him or herself.

Talk about a low profile! This man or woman makes a point of keeping under the radar. Being the center of attention, even at his own parties, makes this individual very uneasy. In fact, he'd rather go unnoticed than let others pay too much attention to him. When he is the object of others' attention, he handles it awkwardly.

> *Everyone loves attention from people they care about. People with thin lower lips are just a lot more selective about the people from whom they will accept it—and how much they will accept.*

As for praise, believe it or not, it can be a real aggravation to this person. He just doesn't know how to accept it gracefully, let alone internalize it in a way that feels good.

This Attention Avoider does like attention and affection from the people he cares about. Everyone does. What's different in this case is that he's much more selective about the people he'll accept it from and when he'll accept it. And he's very definite about how much attention he'll accept, too. People with thin lower lips enjoy some attention from some people, but they don't like or need lots of attention from lots of people. He'll accept and bask (briefly) in your kind remarks if he likes you, but that's about as far as he'll go. Beyond that, your most thoughtful words of praise will fall on deaf ears.

If you buy your narrow-lipped love interest a gift, you might be disappointed in her reaction. It won't always go over as well as you'd hoped. Since gifts show appreciation and this woman is uncomfortable with being appreciated, she may accept it with less *savoir-faire* and grace than you expect to see. You must understand that when someone demonstrates affection to this person, she assumes the giver wants something in return. Suddenly, she feels obligated, a feeling she doesn't enjoy.

This person tends to be an individualist, perhaps even a loner. You'll find she likes keeping a low profile, separating herself from the rest of the world and staying uninvolved. Since she shies away from attention from just about anyone, you're more likely to find her standing back observing people than approaching and initiating contact with others. She certainly doesn't feel comfortable when people actively or overtly try to engage or involve her.

Engaging the Attention Avoider

Don't even try to use this low-level personality trait to engage this individual. It can't be done. He'll probably have many other personality traits written all over his face just screaming out how to approach him and what to say. You'll have much better luck focusing on one of them.

> *Don't be obvious about your interest in him...unless he has already expressed a clear interest in you. Remember also that overtly focusing too much attention on him will make him nervous.*

However, his thin lower lip does tell you a few things to *avoid*. First, even if you're really interested in him, don't be obvious about it unless he has already shown a real interest in you. Avoid overtly focusing lots of attention on him. It'll make him feel uncomfortable with you and may even lead him to want to push you away. Knowing he can't tolerate lots of attention, try showing only limited interest in him at first. Pay him a small compliment, something nice, but not overstated. Then back off. Later on, when you feel he's open to it, approach him again and talk about something you think might interest him. Don't come on too strong. Be relaxed, sincere, even subdued...like he is. In short, demonstrate your attraction to him in subtle ways, so that he doesn't feel pressured to respond in any way.

Second, since this person typically isn't comfortable being the object of too much attention from others, go easy on gifts and other gestures. They may not get you very far—they'll feel like an obligation to her and could easily be perceived as pressure. Instead, she may feel much more comfortable if you just relax and hang back a bit. Try to let your new relationship evolve naturally, giving her a chance to direct her attention and interest toward you for a change. If she can avoid being in the spotlight of your attention, you'll probably find that she'll be a lot more open and receptive to you when your interest isn't too overt.

Do our lips indicate we are a good match?

Now that you know how to read the upper lip and the lower lip, you'll find it very useful to know how different types of lips match up...

Matching large lips

A woman (or man) with a large upper lip loves to show her affection toward others by paying lots of attention to them and communicating freely. When she also has a large lower lip, it means she loves to *receive* attention and acceptance as much as she loves to *give* it. This woman tends to be a very communicative, expressive person. She would be a good match for...

Partner A   **Partner B**

Large lips (needs to give and   *a partner who has similarly*
receive attention) are most   *large lips (has attention needs).*
compatible with...

...a man (or woman) with equally large lips (proportionately). With a large lower lip he can appreciate and enjoy the mountains of attention and acceptance that she (with her large upper lip) will heap on him. At the same time, his large upper lip tells you that he'll enjoy providing the feedback and attention that she needs and wants (as seen in her large lower lip).

Matching large and small lips

Women and men with large upper lips go out of their way to show affection to others and pay attention to them. When they also have a thin or non-existent lower lip, they don't enjoy being the focal point of anyone's attention. Such people are good matches for...

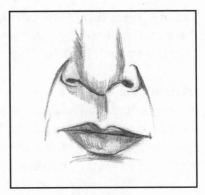

Partner A
Thin lower-lipped and full upper-lipped people match best with...

Partner B
people who have thin upper lips and full lower lips.

...men or women who have thin upper lips and full lower lips, since that indicates they are unlikely to pay attention to others but want to be the object of lots of attention.

Matching small and lips

Men or women who have thin upper and lower lips don't feel they need to give or receive attention from others. They are very much the quiet spectators, the loners. They're good matches for...

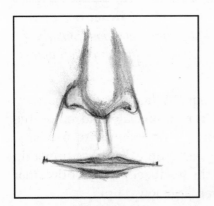

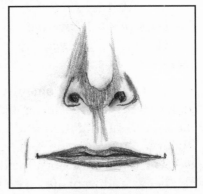

Partner A
Thin-lipped people don't need to give or receive attention, so...

Partner B
they match best with people who have equally small lips.

...others with similarly thin lips who, like them, also have a low-level need to give and receive attention from others.

THE CHIN

Sex, touching and physical relationships—
How to find the special person who matches your needs:

The chin tells you how
physical he or she wants to get.

The deep chin: The touch-driven partner

High-level—The large, deep chin

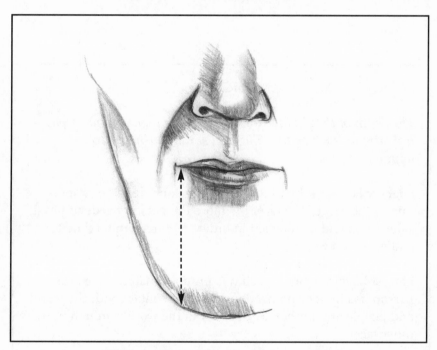

*The longer his chin, the more your mate
enjoys and needs to use touch to relate to
people and the world around him.*

The desire for sex and touching is one of the most important needs you can see on the face of someone to whom you're

attracted. The depth of the chin shows you how significant touching is to your potential partner. The drive to touch and be touched is extremely powerful. At its highest levels it is a potent, constant need that cannot be repressed without consequences.

Just as it sounds, the touch facet is the need to physically touch and be touched by others we care about, the need to communicate in a visceral, physical manner. It's also the need to touch and be touched emotionally. We literally reach out to caress and embrace those people and things we want to know more about. We touch to understand, to gather information about the world around us, to make physical contact and to form a physical bond with others.

Quick Tips

The depth of the chin tells you how much a person needs physical stimuli, such as touching and sexual intimacy, to be happy.

Highest Levels: When the chin is large and deep, in proportion to the rest of the face, the more the person needs to physically touch and be touched in order to understand, relate to and enjoy his world.

Lowest Levels: When the chin is proportionately short, the person has little or no need for physical contact with the world and people around her. She relates to the world through her other facets.

How to measure: Measure the distance from the corner of the mouth down to the bottom of the jaw bone. The longer the distance, the greater the need to touch and to physically bond with others.

Have you ever watched *The Tonight Show* with Jay Leno? If so, then you've seen a high-touch person in action. Jay has a chin that is large and long in proportion to his face, a sure sign that he possesses a powerful need to touch. You can even see evidence of this on the show. He starts each night by shaking hands with the audience. Whenever he wants to demonstrate his affection for a guest, he almost can't keep himself from reaching over to put his hand on their arm or shoulder. What does a High-level Toucher like Jay Leno do for fun? He drives a motorcycle, one of many ways a high-touch person can satisfy his or her need for physical stimuli.

Jay Leno, however, is only one of many high-profile, high-touch people you've seen before. You've probably also seen the faces of Drew Carey, Matt Damon, Ellen Degeneres and Howard Stern, to name just a few.

If you follow contact sports like football, think about (or, better yet, find some pictures of) athletes you know. Most have chins that signal their need for, and love of, physical contact. After all, nothing satisfies a football lineman more than crashing into another person. Nothing is more thrilling to a wrestler than the feeling of the steamy gymnasium, the cool rubber mat and grappling with his opponent. (By the way, you won't usually find this deep-chin trait on tennis players, for instance, since these athletes typically don't need ongoing physical contact.)

Along with the need to touch and physically commune with others, a deep chin reveals the need and ability to care for others. These people love to be needed and want to share with their friends. They strive to be of service and feel fulfilled by caring for others. Usually, deep chin types are also caring, nurturing mothers and fathers.

These individuals' acute sensitivity to touch also means they especially enjoy contact with people, animals and objects of all kinds. By the same token, they absolutely loathe touching (and being touched) by people or things they don't like. A stranger's touch, for example, may be particularly unwelcome to some deep-chin types. Even if it's accidental, it can feel like a violation to them.

Every touch this person makes is very meaningful. So, take note: When your new partner makes a point of touching you, she is demonstrating that she likes you. You have been accepted, she feels comfortable with you and she wants to connect with you on a deeper, more intense level.

A person with a big chin can be very "touchy-feely" on dates or even upon first meeting him. If he likes you and is feeling uninhibited, you'll find that he tends to touch you often, especially when he wants to get your attention or make a point by grasping your sleeve or touching your your hand, arm or shoulder. He may enjoy standing close or even leaning against you. He wants to be close to you, feel you and keep ongoing contact.

> *A High-level Toucher shows she is comfortable with you by touching you. It's her way of demonstrating that she likes you. Her touch is a good clue that you have been accepted and she wants to strengthen her connection with you.*

Since the High-level Toucher has heightened tactile sensitivity, when he or she touches you it usually feels especially pleasant. This individual is generally a gentle creature, at least in the way he or she makes physical contact. If you also have a keen sense of touch, you'll particularly enjoy his or her expressive hugs and kisses.

You'll find high-touch people like to place their hands on everything, animate or inanimate, alike. Holding something and experiencing how it feels tells them volumes about the object of their attention. Watch them when you can, especially if they don't realize you're around. You'll find them running their hands over surfaces that are soft or smooth. You'll see these High-level Touchers feeling the soft textures of their clothing or the suppleness of their own skin. They'll run their hands through their hair. When they're thinking about buying particular items, you'll invariably see them pick the objects up and hold them in their hands to see what they feel like.

By the same token, they become easily irritated or frustrated when they can't touch something (or someone) that's important to them or when they touch things that have an unpleasant texture. They especially dislike having to walk across sandy or dirty floors or wear coarse wool sweaters or handle things that feel unfinished and rough. These are major aggravations to their high-level, highly tactile sense.

> *High-touch individuals are naturally driven to want to touch people and things they like. The problem is that this can be such a strong need it can be very hard to control. Occasionally, their desire to physically touch people is misconstrued, but generally others respond positively to their physicality.*

Touch-sensitive people thrive on the feelings of peace and security they get just from holding onto things. That's why they often surround themselves with pets. They do well with dogs, cats and other animals they can cuddle and stroke.

High-level Touchers frequently are also expert healers, probably because they easily identify with other living things, their situations and their problems. They may not realize it, but often they intuitively know what to do to help the sick and even, in the most dramatic instances, how to heal.

Not surprisingly, few people deal as poorly with rejection as someone with a high need to touch and be touched. This individual cares so much about others that when a person he likes no longer values him, he can go through intense emotional pain. If you find yourself having to end a relationship with someone sporting a big chin, do your best to let him or her down with extreme kindness and sensitivity.

Life can be painful also for people who need touch, but don't have a way to express it. When highly touch-sensitive people aren't able to satisfy this inner drive, because they're not using their tactile sense enough, they can easily lose their mental or emotional balance. By cutting themselves off from this key component of their makeup, even the most secure individuals can quickly lose confidence in themselves. They can even become very antisocial.

High-touch people are naturally driven to want to touch people, animals and things they like. The problem is that this physical reaching out can be such a strong need that, for some, it can be very hard to control. What can you expect if someone with a deep chin likes you? There are two possibilities. If he is feeling confident or encouraged and is not feeling inhibited, you could well find your new friend or partner almost glued to you. If you're not in the mood for this level of contact, this individual may seem overly aggressive. On the other hand, if this high-touch person is inhibited or thinks his physical overtures would be unwelcome, he will hold back...but at a price. It's not uncommon for people with strong but thwarted drives for physical contact to fall back on drinking or drugs to free their inhibitions so they can feel better.

How important are matching chins?

No matter what size chin you have, I can't stress enough how important it is to align yourself with partners who have chins of a proportionally equivalent size as yours. That way, you're both going to be happy in the area of physical intimacy. When both your chins are comparable in size, your partner will want and enjoy the same level of physical contact as you do. When your chin sizes differ markedly, you may very well

> *The most successful matches when it comes to the chin are between partners whose chins are of proportionally equivalent sizes. When chin sizes correspond, partners will find more compatability in the physical side of their relationships, both desiring similar levels of touch.*

both end up unhappy in this important area; one of you will want more sex and physical attention while the other wants less. A relationship will be difficult to sustain when it's subject to this sort of imbalance.

Engaging the High-level Toucher

If you are searching for a satisfying, long-term relationship with the right partner, this is one facial feature, chin size, I'd really recommend you identify and evaluate first. Whatever you do, don't ignore the importance of a mutually satisfying and beneficial sex life.

> *The deep-chin person you're with can easily be encouraged by your touch. They can also, however, misread it as an invitation— even if you mean it only as an innocent, friendly gesture.*

Let's suppose you have a deep chin and you've found someone with a chin that closely matches yours in size. Great. What does that tell you about this individual? You know first-hand how important touching is to your potential partner and that it's a key way for him to gather information about others and the world around him. You also know that if you want to make a good first (and lasting) impression and quickly establish a strong connection, you can do it through physical contact.

Think of touch as a sensory tool, just like your words are verbal tools, that you can use to deepen your communication, to make a point or show your affection. Use physical contact as a way to enhance your friendship and augment your relationship. Show your attractive new friend that you enjoy touch as much as he or she does.

At the same time, be aware of how significant even small physical gestures can be. The deep-chin person can be easily encouraged by your touch. He can also misread a tap on the arm, for example, as an invitation, even if you mean it only as an innocent gesture. If you sense that your touching has been misinterpreted, back off and find other ways to connect with this individual. Otherwise, you run the risk of manipulating or misguiding him, especially if he, too, has a strong touching nature.

Begin a relationship with anyone who has a modest to high need for touch slowly. If you have a high need for touch and you find yourself attracted to someone who also has a high level of this need, you may feel moved (or almost driven) to establish physical contact right away. It would be smarter of you to hold back initially and make sure she is attracted to you before initiating this important connection. Why not let her make the first contact? Otherwise, you may be seen as overly aggressive and your touching will feel like a violation. Once you sense you're both getting along well, it's safe to consider some modest contact.

Holding onto the High-level Toucher

The most successful (and the only satisfying) way to enjoy being with a very touch-sensitive person is to always fill his or her need for physical (and emotional) contact. A High-level Toucher regularly needs and enjoys cuddling, sex, hugging, kissing and plain old touching. Though most everyone enjoys this kind of physical contact, what's different in a High-level Toucher is that he or she needs and wants it constantly. It's very likely that you'll only be able to provide that level of sustained physical connection if you also have an equally high need for touching. If you don't have as great a need for contact as your deep-chinned partner, what at first may feel like wonderful romantic experiences with a well-suited mate can, as time goes on, start to fill you with resentment. Even sex, kissing and hugging will come to feel like chores over time if you begin to view them as excessive.

Small chin: Watch for a thinker

Low-level—A small chin

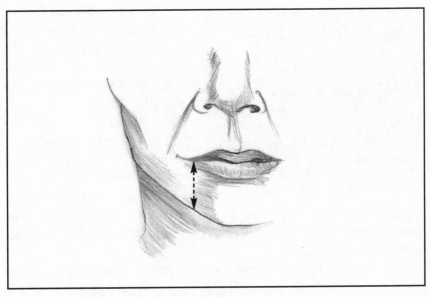

A proportionately small chin indicates that this person may appreciate you more for your mind than your body.

The smaller the chin, the less the need for physical contact. When you find yourself looking at a person with a chin that seems small for his or her face, you can bet you're looking at someone who really doesn't need a lot of physical contact, doesn't think much about touching and doesn't understand its significance to people with proportionately larger chins.

This person has no strong need for sex, hugs, stroking or all those things that physically focused people tend to love so much. When he does connect physically with someone, chances are he won't feel the same intense sensitivity—or attach the same meaning to the experience—as his high-touch counterparts.

Instead of reaching out to touch the world, small-chinned people tend to stay more tightly wrapped within themselves. They don't need much physical contact or intimacy. These Low-level Touchers frequently have no special desire to concern themselves with others. Instead, they tend to express themselves and their feelings mostly in words or through stronger, more pronounced personality traits that they possess.

> *People with small chins tend to stay more within themselves instead of reaching out to "touch" the world. Rather than needing physical contact, they look for more cerebral connections with others.*

When these men and women like other people, it's probably not because they have been physically or emotionally touched by them. More likely, it's because they admire how the others think or they're attracted to their intelligence, senses of humor or other personality traits.

The Low-level Toucher may wonder to herself why she feels no compelling reason to physically connect with others when she sees the world around her engaged in a highly physical sexual dance and seemingly so preoccupied with touching. The truth is, for her, anything more than a modest amount of physical contact is an aggravation, pure and simple.

You'll find the Low-level Toucher doesn't like being needed. She prefers to be independent from others and, unless she is sublimating other issues into her sex drive, she has only a limited, occasional need for hugging, kissing, cuddling, sex and other physical contact.

> *To win over the small-chin individual, instead of trying to further your relationship by getting physical, build a strong and lasting connection by showing that you are a thinking, independent person.*

You might also discover that this individual has little interest in raising a family. The idea of children or other dependents just does not appeal to her. She does have other strong points, however. In addition to the other high-level facets she possesses, you will probably find yourself appreciating her ability to think, to observe or her keen sense of humor. People with smaller chins often have very sharp minds.

Do our chins indicate we are a good match?
Again, just as with large chins, your chins point to a potentially good relationship only if yours is proportionately as small as his or hers. Don't kid yourself here. Be as honest about both of your chin sizes as you can. They need to be very similar in size. Nobody wins when one person requires more physical contact than the other.

Engaging the Low-level Toucher
You'll do best to stand back and bide your time a bit instead of trying to further your budding relationship with a Low-level Toucher through physical contact. Alternatively, establish yourself as a thinking, independent individual. Show him or her the other abilities you possess, especially your more cerebral interests. Impress the Low-level Toucher with your intelligence, logic, your sense of humor or your quick thinking. Since physical contact is sometimes seen as an aggravation to this individual, don't push too hard to get a kiss or a hug at first. Wait until you've known each other longer and then try to match your touching gestures to his or hers. With practice, you will both find the balance between the cerebral and the physical that works for your relationship.

Holding onto the Low-level Toucher
Since this personality facet indicates your friend has limited need in this area, look for other, stronger personality traits revealed by facial features. Discover needs he or she has that you *can* engage and traits that also match your personality.

THE NECK

How to learn if your potential mate won't take "No!" for an answer:

The neck width tells you how stubborn he or she is.

Stubborn or pliable, talkative or attentive: It's all in the neck

High-level—The thick, short neck

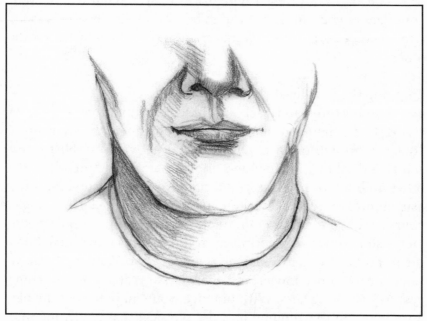

*The short, thick neck individual is truly stubborn
and far from the world's best listener.*

Most features on the face are signposts to our essential personality *needs*. They show our need to be critical, our need to touch, our need to manage, our need to dream or whatever.

Not the neck. The neck is an indicator not so much of needs, but of a person's style of behavior. It tells you how he or she acts.

In this section, we're going to look at the meaning of the four most common shapes of necks you will see so that you can determine whether that appealing person is really a good match.

Quick Tips

The size and shape of the neck tells you the level of the person's determination, as well as his or her ability to listen.

Highest Levels: When the neck is short and thick, the person tends to be stubborn and a poor listener.

Lowest Levels: When the neck is long and thin, the person is a good listener and flexible in her thinking.

How to measure: Study the length and thickness of the neck, from the point where it meets the jaw to where it meets the shoulders.

The short, thick neck

The most obvious trait you'll notice in the man or woman with a short, thick neck is that he is stubborn. Determined to get his or her way, this person fights for what he or she wants above all else. Such an individual steadfastly stands up for preserving his or her own rights and ideas, regardless of the obstacles. This person simply must be Number One; he or she must achieve First Place. Second Place is not acceptable.

Not surprisingly, people with short, thick necks often rise to positions of power and stature in their respective fields. People such as Mikhail Gorbachev, Kenneth Starr, Jesse Jackson, Winston Churchill, Alfred Hitchcock and Al Roker are known for tenaciously adhering to their goals and ideals, even if it takes their entire lives, to reach them.

It's not an exaggeration to say that virtually nothing changes this individual's mind and he is usually locked into his own ideas. Or that he only says and does things when he's ready. He frequently sees only the black and white of issues, rarely the gray areas.

When you're around him, you may feel as if you and your opinions don't count. You're not alone. If you were to ask his friends and acquaintances (and if you got honest answers), you'd find that a lot of people share that feeling.

You'll find he has a hard time with people who try to change his ideas or who interrupt him or, worst of all, disagree with him. So be warned! Deal with him gingerly. Don't take him on too directly or you'll lose.

If you like to talk, you'll probably have to struggle to be heard. He is a very good talker himself, along with being a poor listener. This individual can chatter on all day without much concern for what you want, your attitudes or your concerns...until he's said his piece. You will find that he enjoys dominating conversations. He also has a bad habit of butting into conversations, something you'll either have to live with or learn to overlook.

Talk about stubborn! It's a major event when he changes his mind. Plus, he has a very hard time admitting when he's wrong. (He must clearly see his error before he'll 'fess up to anything.)

Short, thick neck men and women enjoy dominating conversations. They also have the bad habit of butting into conversations, something you'll either have to live with or learn to overlook if you choose them as your mates.

And on the good side? Since he doesn't bend and he doesn't compromise, you can't find a more dependable, solid, persevering and persistent person. If you're looking for an advocate or someone to run interference for you or lead the charge to get something done, he's someone you can count on.

What's more, this person loves challenges. No matter how huge the obstacle, he'll tackle it because in his mind nothing can stop him.

Do our necks indicate we are a good match?

Since she likes to talk and is usually quite rigid and inflexible, your neck had better be at least a little longer and a little narrower if you want a satisfying relationship. (Keep reading to find out why.)

Engaging the stubborn talker

It's very simple: Just let him talk. Ask an occasional question and let him answer. Give him your views about a topic and stand back while he counters with his. You can't change his mind and you certainly can't contradict him without pushing him away. So relax and just let him be himself. If you've got the right kind of neck, you might just be a perfect fit.

Holding onto the stubborn talker

Find things she cares about and give her challenges. Be willing to play second chair. Learn to enjoy the art of careful listening. As long as you're sincerely willing to let her run things (at least what she considers the important things), you two will be a good match in this area.

Though still stubborn, he actually listens

High level—The short, thin neck

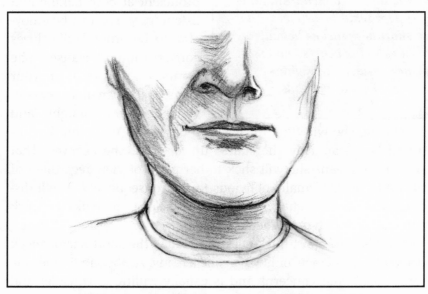

Although a good listener, a person with a short,
thin neck tends to be stubborn and unchanging.

Men and women with short, narrow necks are a great deal like people with short, thick necks. They share the same need for being in First Place. They have the same stubborn, rigid, "I'm-never-going-to-change" quality. But there is one important difference: The person with a thinner neck is usually willing to listen to others.

Why? Because unlike her short-thick-neck counterpart, she's open to other people's ideas. She wants to broaden her understanding and knowledge and to continually reevaluate her point of view on a wide variety of issues that are important to her.

What's interesting about this individual is that, for all her listening and openness, she is inflexible and usually won't change her mind even when other less stubborn people would. You'll find that she probably has a habit of changing her thinking—temporarily—but the next time you see her you can almost bet she'll be right back espousing the belief or point of view she had originally.

> *The short, thin necked person loves conversation because he wants your ideas. But no matter how convincing they are, he will fight for his own opinions, staunchly standing up for what he believes. That short neck means he will stick to his beliefs and what he considers his rights—regardless of the odds.*

This person is quite proficient at both talking and listening, so she can be enjoyable to be around. She loves conversation because she wants an infusion of your ideas. Still, no matter how convincing others' thoughts and beliefs are, she will fight for her own opinions. You might be surprised how staunchly she stands up for what she believes. That short neck means she will stick to her point of view regardless of the odds. She's virtually oblivious to the consequences. You'll discover that she loves challenges, too, but she's far more likely to pick and choose which ones she takes on.

Like the short-thick-neck individual, the short-narrow-neck person talks and acts only when she's ready. At the same time, she cares about your concerns and is usually willing to consider and perhaps adopt your views as her own, if only temporarily.

Engaging (and holding onto) the stubborn listener

Your best bet here is to be conversational. Find things to discuss that you are both interested in and then just start talking. Don't expect to sell your ideas, at least not permanently. Instead, just enjoy sharing them whether they are accepted or not.

Over the long haul, the two things that will help your relationship in this area are sharing your ideas and your being willing to be flexible in the face of his or her inflexibility. After all, few things fuel this person's spirit more than dealing with others who also like to share ideas, but, at the same time, respect the stubborn listener's need to maintain his or her own beliefs and ideas.

If you like to talk, this one's for you... just don't expect an answer!

High-level—The long, narrow neck

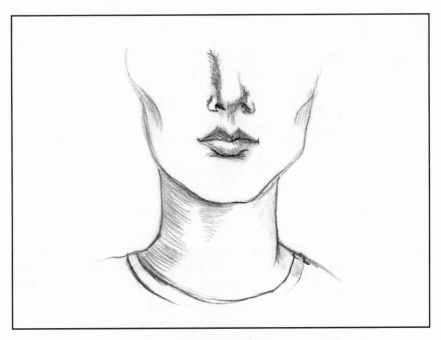

People with long and thin necks are very flexible and great listeners! However, they often have little to say, leaving others in a one-sided conversation.

Courtney Cox, Lisa Kudrow, Lauren Holly, Cindy Crawford and Julia Roberts are people with long, graceful necks. If your new love interest has this feature, he or she has something in common with these celebrities. Around people with long, thin necks, you'll find yourself talking more because you're in the company of the world's best listeners.

What's more, long and narrow necks belong to people who are truly flexible and who naturally and willingly bend over backwards to meet others' desires and expectations. They change their beliefs, plans, ideas and desires to suit their current situations and what other people want. They are as pliable as you'll find, being people who prefer to go along with you and your suggestions rather than stubbornly going their own ways.

A long, narrow-necked individual is usually very patient. Often patently agreeable and willing to follow your lead, she also gets along well with almost everyone. In fact, she wants to get along with every last man, woman and child on the planet and it probably bothers her that she can't.

> *The long, narrow-necked person is a good listener. She absorbs ideas like a sponge. So when faced with repeatedly hearing others put forth their convictions, she may decide her ideas aren't worth much.*

Her long neck tells you she is also a great listener. She loves to just sit and absorb whatever you have to say and can be good at getting conversations started by asking a simple open-ended question that, she hopes, will prompt a much longer answer from you. And she'll keep asking prompting questions just so you talk and she can listen. Spend a few hours with her and you'll suddenly realize that you've done all the talking. Don't worry. That's fine with her.

A person with a long and narrow neck fits into just about any group, any setting. He's usually well liked because people enjoy the way he pays such focused attention to them.

As a good listener, he absorbs ideas like a sponge, internalizing them quickly and often adopting them as his own. In the face of others' certainty and their relentless talking, he may decide that his own ideas aren't worth much. That's why he can often be easily impressed by others and can be persuaded to do many things as long as they don't contradict his core values.

Engaging and holding onto the flexible listener

Obviously, if your new love interest is one of these people, you'll want to enjoy chatting...and chatting...and chatting. Don't expect him to open up to you if you start asking questions. It won't work.

Repeated attempts to get him to talk will almost guarantee you'll aggravate him and will eventually end what could have been a long, intimate conversation leading to a closer relationship.

You'll probably have to jump in and take the lead and let him follow. Chances are, he'll like it when you take charge and let him join in. If you want to, you might probe a bit and find out how he feels about himself. See where he's feeling insecure and make a few positive casual remarks that build him up and show that you enjoy his company. Allow him to keep a lower profile or at least don't call too much attention to him.

It may take more time for you to get to know that special person with a long, narrow neck than you'd like. In fact, he or she tends to be so reticent and holds back so much that his or her true self is only known by close friends, not new acquaintances. This person is inclined to take a backseat, substituting his or her own true self, ideas, desires, goals and much more with someone else's.

A good conversationalist, but stubborn

High level—The long, thick neck

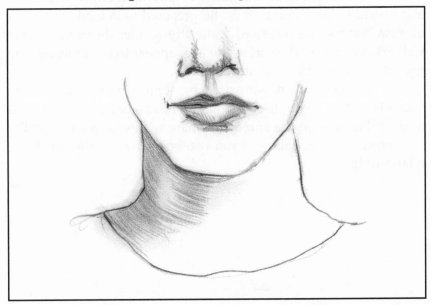

Necks that are long and thick belong to people who are both good talkers and listeners, yet are also very stubborn.

Long- and thick-necked men and women are interesting, seemingly almost contradictory combinations of attentive listening on the one hand and, on the other, fighting spirits and aggressiveness that others often admire. A number of famous people who share this feature include Senator Bill Bradley, Jimmy Hoffa, Bob Dole and Al Gore.

Compare the personality of a long, thick-necked individual with a short, narrow-necked individual and you will see some similarities. While Short-narrow enjoys talking (indicated by the short neck length), Long-thick neck is a better listener.

At the same time, he's different from people with long and thin necks because, even though he loves to listen, he's not nearly as pliable. A strong advocate for his rights, beliefs and goals, this aggressive conversationalist will stand up for himself in the face of virtually any obstacles. Ultimately, he may end up changing his mind and going along with you, but not without a fight for what he believes in.

Engaging and holding onto the aggressive conversationalist

If you like to talk, you and your long, thick necked interest will be a good match. Engage this individual by putting forward your ideas and watching how he responds. Be prepared to defend your point of view. You may be surprised at the strength he shows in his convictions because on the surface he may appear to be someone who just sits back and takes whatever comes.

You also may be surprised by something else if he likes your ideas: You could discover that he has valuable thoughts and ideas of his own on the subject to share with you. Such a quality may prove very appealing as you two begin a mutually satisfying relationship.

PART 5

Practice Reading People's Faces

If I asked you to analyze the face of a man or woman to whom you were attracted a few days before you read this book, you probably couldn't. You've learned a great deal since then. You now have at your disposal the keys to uncovering dozens of traits and attributes which will help you know whether that special someone is the right person for you.

This section is an opportunity to see just how much you've learned and put it into practice. Reading and doing the practice analyses here will help you in many ways. First, you'll see how to do an analysis based on the twelve facial features you now know. More importantly, you'll see how facial features show up in many ways, often appearing slightly different from the more extreme illustrations included in the preceding chapters. In real life you'll find that most features, in fact, are somewhere between the high-level extreme and the low-level extreme we have talked about to this point. After reading and studying this section, you'll be able to better determine how to categorize your love interest's facial features into high-level, mid-level or low-level.

You'll also see how you can combine what you know about one personality trait with another and thus learn even more about him or her. You'll see more clearly how you can apply what you now know in your interactions with your romantic partners.

Next, you'll become more sensitive to possible pitfalls you can avoid, including how photographs can make reading faces more challenging...how smiles completely distort the facial features and make them more difficult to read accurately...and how plastic surgery or even plucking one's eyebrows can throw off your analyses.

Finally, you'll use your new skills to analyze three couples. After analyzing both partners, we'll see where their individual personality traits successfully complement each other as well as where they are not especially well matched.

You will find this section a short but important springboard to your immediate and long-term success in finding and relating to the special people in your life. It will also help you feel comfortable taking your new skills into the world and using them on the real, live people you interact with every day.

How to proceed

You can approach this section in two ways. First, you may simply want to read the analyses following the pictures and learn additional information about what I see in these faces. If you're feeling confident about your abilities, another way to benefit from this section is to do your own analysis on each person and then compare your conclusions with mine. Since you're just beginning to read faces, this route may seem a bit daunting. Don't let it be. It's really okay to make mistakes and even let yourself get a bit discouraged occasionally as long as you keep practicing. That's the process I went through while learning and it served me well. By taking a chance and risking making mistakes—in this section or out in public—you'll quickly find out what you know and what you don't. Refer back to the previous section of the book as often as necessary. At this point, your accuracy is not *nearly* as important as your willingness to get started. And I guarantee that with practice you can only get better and better.

Couple Number One—Who are they...and are they a good match?

Photo © David Katzenstein/CORBIS

Questions to ask yourself when analyzing the faces of this couple:

1. Wide or narrow forehead?
2. Close or elevated eyebrows?
3. Rounded or flat upper eyelids?
4. Pointed or wide nose tip?
5. Full or thin upper lip?
6. Deep or shallow chin?
7. Tight eyelid or loose and fleshy?
8. Wide or narrow distance between facial creases?
9. Rounded or flat lower eyelids?
10. Mouth curves up or down?
11. Big and full or thin lower lip?
12. Thick or thin neck? Long or short?

Ready to get started? Then take a deep breath, relax and start to scan the man's face in the picture.

Ask yourself, "What features that we've studied stand out?" Which of the features get your attention? Which seem disproportionately large or small, wide or narrow. Which are high- or low-level?

After you've spotted the more apparent traits, ask yourself what other, less obvious, facial features are telling you.

Finally, what other characteristics about this person's personality can you deduce by combining what you know about two (or more) facets?

Begin working on your own analysis. Once you've finished, continue reading below to compare your results with mine.

Peering inside the man

When I look at this handsome man, the first thing I notice is his strong, deep chin (see question #6). Even though he is smiling (which distorts its size) his chin appears to be large in proportion to the rest of his face. It signals that he relates to his world more through touch than through many of his other senses. He's definitely going to want a physical relationship.

My attention now turns to his low, curving eyebrows, eyebrows that clearly hug his eyes (question #2). These tell me he is someone who jumps into his relationships and attaches himself to the object of his attention. People probably find him very warm and friendly.

How would you size up his forehead (#1)? Is it wide or narrow? My view is that it's a higher-level facet, on the wider side. Therefore, I'd surmise that he has a strong personality and that he usually would want to take charge of the relationship, though not always.

The next feature that stands out are his large round eyes. He appears to be someone who is constantly curious, seeking new adventures and trying new things. He is obviously very compassionate toward people and other living things (#3). Plus, he is careful not to take risks or do anything that might harm his image or his physical self (#9).

Notice the lips. Both are larger, higher-level facets, yet not extraordinarily large for his face. His lower lip (#11) is on the fuller side and slightly larger than his upper lip, so we know he enjoys the limelight and the attention of others. The size of his upper lip (#5), while not as full as its lower counterpart, is large, yet still in proportion to the rest of the face. Therefore he is probably a bit talkative and enjoys others' attention, but these are not high-level traits; he isn't consumed with the constant need to talk and seek others' acceptance.

Let's skip over to the nose and look at his need (ability) to criticize others (#4). His nose tip is on the narrower side, suggesting he is one to criticize occasionally, but not as constantly as a very pointed-nosed person. Which one of these two people, the man or the woman, do you think is going to be more critical? Which one will feel more judged?

How idealistic is he (#8)? Is he driven to improve the world? Not far from it. The skin between the two creases that traverse his cheek looks narrow. You would most likely find him a competitive sort, perhaps even driven to realize some huge, unattainable dreams.

Check out his need for control and discipline (#7). His level of control is quite high, as evidenced by the fine, thin line at the juncture of his upper eyelid and the skin above. He doesn't show the very highest control level (usually evidenced by the skin cutting sharply across the corner of the outer eye), but it's higher than a low-level trait nonetheless. I'd bet that, between his need for control and his need to manage, he dominates most relationships in which he is involved.

How do you determine his level of stubbornness (#12) when you can't see his entire neck? In truth, you can't, but you can assume one thing: His neck is probably not especially long since his shirt collar is large enough to cover it completely, and we learned a short neck indicates a poor listener.

That's my assessment of this man. How was yours? Was it similar to mine? If not, don't get discouraged. Remember, I have the advantage of almost thirty years of face reading experience behind me.

Peering inside the woman

Observing this woman's attractive face, I first notice her wide nose (#4). The telltale tip is obviously wide. Therefore, to the question, "How much does she feel she needs to improve (criticize) others?" I'd say almost never. This is clearly a low-level trait. She is not critical at all and is much more willing to let people be who they are, flaws and all.

Next I notice her forehead (#1) which is both high and quite wide. Be careful here. To read the width accurately, don't measure at the front hairline. You have to look at the forehead width back a little farther, past the hairline. This tells us that she has about the same need to manage their relationship as her partner, perhaps even a stronger need.

Her eyebrows (#2) show obvious detachment. Here's a woman who stands back from people and situations, careful not to get too involved. Of these two, despite her smile, she's the person, people might say, who could appear cool and unfriendly, and might even seem less committed to the relationship.

Next, notice the place where her eyelids join with the skin above (#7). You'll see that the juncture forms a crisp, curved line, a clear sign this lady tends to be controlling and to be fairly self-controlled. In this regard, she is similar to her partner, able to hide behind a facade wearing any face she wants.

We already know that touch is very important to her partner, but how important is it to her? Though her smile makes it difficult to assess, her chin (#6) appears balanced and in proportion to her face. She will likely not desire the same level of physicality and touching in the relationship as her mate.

Next, notice her eyes. The rounded lower eyelid (#9) indicates she has a pretty strong, protective concern for herself. She watches out for her reputation and avoids any chance of harm. Compare that with her upper eyelid (#3) which has only a slight curve as it approaches the side of the head. What does that tell you? This is a clear sign that most of the time it's her nature to put her own welfare and interests ahead of others' concerns.

How would you rate her on the idealism scale (#8)? I'd put her at the high end, about the same as her partner, as the skin between the facial creases is narrow on both of them. She, too, has big dreams to fulfill.

And her lips? Since she's smiling, it's hard to make any hard-and-fast conclusions here, particularly about her upper lip. However, her full lower lip (#11) suggests she enjoys the attention others offer her. Her somewhat smaller upper lip (#5) tells us she is less willing to go out of her way to get that attention. If you wanted to step out on a limb, you also might forecast that she isn't inclined to give her partner all the attention he needs.

Finally, what about her levels of determination (#12) and optimism? I confess I wouldn't even take a guess here as her neck, unlike her partner's, is completely covered up.

While we can't predict the future, we can draw some general conclusions about the compatibility of this couple. For one, we discovered they both have high needs for control and to manage themselves and others. To make things work, they will have to learn to compromise, or one of them will have to let the other take control. Since this is a high-level trait in both partners, neither of the previous two options will be easy. While she appears relatively compassionless and primarily concerned for herself and her own needs, he, on the other hand, comes across as very caring and compassionate. Though these two natures could complement one another, his strong need for attention would strain the relationship. Furthermore, her need to stay detached and uninvolved in her relationships, would likely frustrate him; he tends to quickly immerse and commit himself in his relationships. Additionally, his high-level need for touch and a physical relationship will not be fulfilled by her; she wants to keep her distance. Further tension could result from their competitive natures.

Overall, though a few traits seem compatible, many incompatible high-level traits would cause a great deal of conflict and friction in the relationship. I'd say these two are not a good match and if they did become romantically involved, they would probably not have a lasting relationship.

Couple Number Two—Who are they...and are they a good match?

Photo © Cydney Conger/CORBIS

Questions to ask yourself when analyzing the faces of this couple:

1. Wide or narrow forehead?
2. Close or elevated eyebrows?
3. Rounded or flat upper eyelids?
4. Pointed or wide nose tip?
5. Full or thin upper lip?
6. Deep or shallow chin?
7. Tight eyelid or loose and fleshy?
8. Wide or narrow distance between facial creases?
9. Rounded or flat lower eyelids?
10. Mouth curves up or down?
11. Big and full or thin lower lip?
12. Thick or thin neck? Long or short?

I like to begin my analysis by pointing out the most prominent features. Which features get your attention? Which seem disproportionately large or small, wide or narrow? Which are high-level, which are low-level?

Now, what do the rest of the less obvious facial features tell you? Can you draw any conclusions by combining what you know about two (or more) facets? Keep these questions in mind as you do your analysis. Read on to see what I have concluded about the personalities of these two individuals.

Peering inside the man

Looking first at the male I ask myself, how wide is his forehead (#1)? The answer to this may be a little trickier than it seems, for two reasons. First, two-dimensional photos can easily exaggerate some features while almost reshaping others. I've found foreheads in particular can suffer distortion in pictures. Second, notice this young man's hairline. He has hair on the sides of his head that is hiding the places we would optimally want to measure. In other words, his forehead appears narrower than it really is. Third, his forehead grows wider the further back on the head it goes. Having said all that, I would say his need to manage is a mid- to moderately high-level need. Of these two individuals, he is the one to most likely want to make the decisions.

My focus next shifts to his eyes. I find these particularly revealing. He has no prominent eyelids, yet look at the skin above the eye: This smooth, tight skin is the sign of a high control person with high-level control needs (#7).

Now look at the curve of his eyes. He has a personality split here. The upper edge (#3) of his right eye (on our left) is gently curved, telling us he sometimes has a moderate sense of compassion for others. His left eye's upper edge (on our right) is "flatter," indicating that at other times he has much less concern for others in his life.

The "flat" shape of his lower eyelids (#9) doesn't seem to vary from side to side, therefore, I would say that he has only a moderate degree of concern for himself. You might call him a risk taker. When we compare top and bottom eyelids, they are roughly the same level of curvature. That means he typically balances the needs of others with his own needs, but doesn't take particularly good care of either himself or his friends and loved ones.

Speaking of his friends and loved ones, he probably has many, given the way his eyebrows run close to his eyes. He is the kind of person who is totally committed and involved in whatever he chooses to do and deeply involved in his relationships (#2). Notice, however, that his eyebrows rise slightly as they approach the side of the head. You can be sure that this guy will grow less attached and more distant in his relationships over the course of time.

How do you rank his chin? I'd say here's a person who has a healthy interest in physical contact (#6). It's not as great a drive as, say, Jay Leno, but it's still a high-level trait.

His upper lip (#5) is very slim, isn't it? So, you know he is not one for lavishing lots of praise and attention on others (no matter how loving he may look). Now, check out his partner's lower lip. Do you think she needs more than he'll give her? Probably.

His lower lip is larger than his upper lip, but still isn't huge (#11). Overall, you'll find him a pretty quiet person. If you're someone with large lips (like his partner), you probably won't get the attention, feedback and interaction from him you desire.

Based on the creases on his cheeks, his sense of idealism appears to be low to moderate, suggesting he doesn't feel the need to have huge dreams or high mountains to conquer, nor does he particularly need to compete against others (#8).

That doesn't mean he's always contented. He also has quite a pointed nose. This is a red flag indicating that, by nature, he has a need to improve others (and himself) by judging or criticizing them (#4). If you became one of his friends and he cared about you, you would probably find him eager to point out ways you could improve.

Unfortunately, the rest of the features we've studied are difficult to read in this photograph. Since he is smiling, it's difficult to say if he is an optimist (#10). We can't see his neck, so I can only hazard a guess about his neck shape and size (#12). If we could see it clearly, I suspect it would be moderately short and thick. If my suspicion is correct, he is a stubborn talker with poor listening skills. Before we move on, take another look at our female subject's face. See if you can spot the features that would indicate high- and low-level traits from. Now let's analyze her face.

Peering inside the woman

What do you notice first when you look at this nice-looking face? Immediately, I see the large, relatively round eyes. Our female subject, quite unlike her partner, is obviously someone who cares about other people as well as herself. The shape of her upper eyelids (#3) is noticeably curved, clearly an indication of her concern for the welfare of both her friends and strangers alike. Her equally round lower eyelid (#9) shows that, despite her interest in others, she does not overlook her own needs. In her relationships, she most likely enjoys caring for her partner and makes sure her needs are taken care of, too.

How about her eyebrows (#2)? They both sit high above her eyes and grow away from her eyes the farther out they go. Whenever you see such ascending eyebrows, you should suspect that the person has a hard time committing herself to a relationship and that close, involved intimacy would be even less likely the longer the relationship continues. Compare her eyebrows with her mate's. She's probably not a great match for him in this area, given his constant need for close attachments and the likelihood she will grow somewhat more distant from her partner than he will.

I hesitate to measure this woman's level of control, since the lighting in the photo makes her eyelids difficult to see (#7). I suspect, however, that it is high, that she is one of those people who has both round eyes and high control at the same time. If we could clearly see the juncture of her eyelid with the skin above, we could say for sure.

How would you rank her level of idealism (#8)? It appears to me to be higher than his. (I guess you could call her a "wide-eyed idealist.")

Unlike her partner, her forehead is easy to read because it doesn't grow wider the farther back it goes (#1); it stays about the same width from front to back. She appears to have a lower- to mid-level need to be in charge, slightly less than her mate.

Look carefully and you'll see that the tip of her nose is moderately wide (#4). Can you guess who'll be the more critical person in this relationship?

Hers are not especially thin lips either, although her smile may be throwing off what her mouth actually says about her. Her larger upper lip (#5) tells us she is someone who probably likes to converse and often goes out of her way to get attention. Her lower lip (#11), even larger than the upper lip, tells us she sincerely loves to be noticed and values whatever affection she gets from others.

Her chin (#6) is not as large as her partner's, although we have to be careful because of her broad smile. Still, in terms of how well they match up, it appears he will be more interested in the physical side of their relationship than she will.

Finally, if you had a better look at her neck, what do you think you'd see (#12)? I strongly suspect we'd see a neck that is both long and narrow. If that's true, she will be the listener in this relationship.

What do you think? Is this couple a good match? Form your own conclusions before reading mine.

This couple could encounter a few difficulties in the relationship. First, her full lower lip shows she requires more attention from (and lots of verbal interaction with) her mate than he, with his narrow upper lip, appears able to give. Second, his eyebrows indicate he is a person who will stay deeply committed to his mate. Her eyebrows show she will be detached from the relationship, growing more aloof as time passes.

In other ways, even though some of their lower-level traits differ, they could still be compatible. For instance, he has a moderate need to control and manage, while her need to be the decision maker is less. He appears to have stronger needs in the area of physical bonding, but hers are not so low as to cause major difficulties. Her neck, long and slender, tells us that she is a good listener, pliable and agreeable, with a tendency to go along with others. This trait can mesh well with his. He has both an inclination to be insistent, if not stubborn, which he displays in his short, thick neck, as well as a need to be in charge as indicated by his wide forehead.

Couple Number Three—Who are they...and are they a good match?

Questions to ask yourself when analyzing the faces of this couple:

1. Wide or narrow forehead?
2. Close or elevated eyebrows?
3. Rounded or flat upper eye-lids?
4. Pointed or wide nose tip?
5. Full or thin upper lip?
6. Deep or shallow chin?
7. Tight eyelid or loose and fleshy?
8. Wide or narrow distance between facial creases?
9. Rounded or flat lower eye-lids?
10. Mouth curves up or down?
11. Big and full or thin lower lip?
12. Thick or thin neck? Long or short?

Ready for your final book-based practice session? This pic-ture gives us two side-by-side faces that may make our feature comparisons simpler.

This time, instead of looking at each person individually, let's look at both people simultaneously and compare their facial appearances. Ask yourself questions like: What features appear nearly the same on both people? What features are different? Then we can again decide after looking at this couple's features, how we think they might get along.

Let's get started...

Comparing their features

Analyzing this couple, I'd start by discussing their nose tips (#4). What do you see? Hers is narrow while his is considerably wider, however he has a very prominent vertical crease running right up the middle. Remember that a crease means this person has developed a strong need (and ability) to criticize. So even though his nose tip is wide, he will be just as willing to point out her failings as she, with her narrow-tip nose, will be.

Now look at their eyebrows (#2). They are noticeably different. His are close to the eyes indicating a strong need to jump into relationships and commitments to people. Hers are at the other end of the spectrum, sitting higher above the eyes. As in our last couple, she will be the person who has the hard time committing to relationships...and she possibly won't seem to grow any closer over time.

We can see levels of control in this photograph rather well. His upper eyelids (#7) are typical of a person with high-level control needs. See how the skin over his outer eyelid pulls across the eye at an angle, removing much of the curve to the eyelid? That skin is also tight and thin. Compare that with his mate. The skin above her upper eyelid is fleshier and there is no crisp line between eyelid and the skin above. Bottom line: You'll find him secretive and mysterious, with a strong, constant need to control things. A supreme actor, he is able to hide his true feelings and wear any face he chooses. She, on the other hand, is by nature someone who acts totally consistently with who she is and likes everything out in the open.

How do their eyes compare? They're not radically different. His upper eyelids (#3) are only slightly rounded, while hers, moderately rounded, reveal her more compassionate nature. Their lower eyelids (#9)—his and hers—appear to be "flat," suggesting that both of them put others' needs ahead of their own. Since her upper eyelids are rounder, we can tell she is the kind of person who sacrifices her own needs for others. She is a true giver while he is more likely to care somewhat less about others, as well as himself.

I see more idealism in his face than hers (#8). He'll be the dreamer and competitor in this relationship.

At first blush, this man and woman have very similar lips, don't they? But take another look. His are actually slightly smaller than hers and, relative to his considerably larger face, must be considered even thinner. I'd say his upper lip (#5) is low level while hers is closer to mid-level. She is more likely to want to connect with the people in her life, while he's more inclined to pull back.

Likewise, his lower lip is proportionately smaller than hers (#11). Again, she is likely to be the person in this relationship to need and expect more attention and affectionate gestures.

How about their chins (#6)? On an absolute basis, his chin is larger than hers. It's also large compared with the rest of his face, while her chin is in proportion to her face. In other words, of the two, he will have a somewhat stronger need for physical connection than she will. Make no mistake, however, she has a healthy need for touching. It's just not as strong and near-constant as his.

We can get a sense of his optimism from our picture (#10). When I see people who are wearing slight smiles like this, if I see the mouth curve up at the ends (as his does), I bet on optimism. Notice how her mouth doesn't turn up despite her faint smile. My guess is that she is neither an optimist nor a pessimist.

I have to admit I have trouble reading their foreheads. The angle of their heads adds to the difficulty. However, we can make educated guesses. Her head is fairly wide, right? That would mean her forehead should also be wide unless her head is oval. While it *does* narrow somewhat, I think you can safely assume that she has a need to manage that's above average. His face, on the other hand, is longer and also seems to narrow slightly as it rises. I'd put his need to take charge in the middle of the spectrum, neither especially high nor low.

Based solely on the 12 features we have been talking about— one-fifth of the total of sixty features included in this method—my guess is that these two individuals would not be a great match for each other. Why? They have just too many key personality traits that are incompatible. For example, both partners are by nature critical people and will find themselves wanting to constantly improve their partners. Also, when one partner seeks out close interaction and needs involvement while the other prefers more independence and reacts adversely to close attachments, friction often results. Finally, in this case we have one person who has a high need for control while his partner has just as strong a need to take charge of everything. Given that these are fairly strong needs, one of them is always going to feel at odds with the other. Here are two people who, according to their faces, might want to keep looking for more suitable partners.

It's your turn

There you have it—a good, basic road map, a decoder, for reading the person to whom you're attracted and unveiling what lies deep within that congregation of features we call a face. You can now instantly identify twelve important personality traits, qualities that have important bearings on your relationships—just from looking at that person's face.

You've come a long way. So far, in fact, that now, when you meet someone you judge special, you probably won't see just his or her face anymore. You may already be zeroing in on the rich treasure chest of abilities, needs, drives, tendencies, wants and behaviors that make that individual either right or not right for you.

If you haven't already, it's time to put your new skills to use. Believe it or not, you're ready to try your new reading abilities on the attractive individual you already know or will soon meet. Use your newly acquired skill to see if he or she is a Mr. or Ms. Right.

Have fun with it. After all, Psycho-Graphicology can be interesting, enlightening and most of all enjoyable, both for you and for that special someone. As I've said before, the more effort you put into reading his or her face, the more chance you'll have to gain and keep the relationship you want. Congratulations! You have now acquired a simple, fast and highly accurate way to assess the *real* person behind the face drawing you to him or her.

Index